Overthinking

Learn How to Break Free of Overthinking, Be Yourself and Build Mental Toughness Using Fast Success Habits and Meditation. Declutter Your Mind, Discover Mindfulness for Creativity and Slow Down Your Brain

RAY SMITH

PUBLISHED BY: Green Book Publishing LTD

58 Warwick Road

London W5 5PX

First Print 2021

Green Book Publishing ®

Legal & Disclaimer

The information contained in this book and its contents is not designed to replace or take the place of any form of medical or professional advice; and is not meant to replace the need for independent medical, financial, legal or other professional advice or services, as may be required. The content and information in this book has been provided for educational and entertainment purposes only.

The content and information contained in this book has been compiled from sources deemed reliable, and it is accurate to the best of the Author's knowledge, information and belief. However, the Author cannot guarantee its accuracy and validity and cannot be held liable for any errors and/or omissions.

Further, changes are periodically made to this book as and when needed. Where appropriate and/or necessary, you must consult a professional (including but not limited to your doctor, attorney, financial advisor or such other professional advisor) before using any of the suggested remedies, techniques, or information in this book.

Upon using the contents and information contained in this book, you agree to hold harmless the Author from and against any damages, costs, and expenses, including any legal fees potentially resulting from the application of any of the information provided by this book. This disclaimer applies to any loss, damages or injury caused by the use and application, whether directly or indirectly, of any advice or information presented, whether for breach of contract, tort, negligence, personal injury, criminal intent, or under any other cause of action.

You agree to accept all risks of using the information presented inside this book.

You agree that by continuing to read this book, where appropriate and/or necessary, you shall consult a professional (including but not limited to your doctor, attorney, or financial advisor or such other advisor as needed) before using any of the suggested remedies, techniques, or information in this book.

Table of Contents

Introduction

'Come to think of it. What would you call the biggest problem people have today?'

I have raised that question in the middle of counseling sessions, intellectual discussions, and seminars that I have been invited to give a talk, and now it's your turn to think over it. I always get responses as you would guess, a few people would put their hands up and comment, "I think it is money," "it has got to be jobs," "crescendo rise in technology," "it is spouse, family" and so on. Most of the time, the responses spin around those points, and I am always amused because none of the answers is right. You can imagine the look on their faces when I tell them that.

The biggest problem in the universe today is not what you were thinking; it is 'overthinking.' We think too hard about everything, and that is why nothing seems moderate today. You are probably one of those who think money, your partner, job, self-confidence and so on are the biggest problems of man, but guess what? You got it wrong because you were 'overthinking' about the issue. You couldn't stop for a second and query yourself, "aren't we overthinking on this planet?", you would rather go for bigger solutions. In most cases, the answer is always closer than you thought, but you were busy nosing far off references. That is a joke, but there could be some point in it.

A human is a burdened being that faces a lot of distress each day. These troubles range from personal or self to family or relationship and career or professional development. None of them should be snubbed for sure, but the biggest and most influencing problems come from personal or self-development. You can't do much with your life if everything isn't right up in your head, and of course, your heart. Yet, with a little support, life expects everyone to get on their feet against these problems. Is that even possible?

Too many people are forced to think out of the sanity box today, and they don't even know it. But overthinking has its dark sides that we can't afford. We risk having a world of mentally unstable kids, teenagers, parents, and leaders, and we mustn't let that happen.

Take a look at your kids; the overthinking ones are always apparent. She would keep asking you when the sky would fall on everyone or what would happen if it does. He would keep imagining he might turn an X-Man someday, and he would try to live like it. Other times, she would moodily sit and ask you how you would save her if someone blows her school up. A young nephew once asked me, "Uncle, what would happen if an Australian red snake coiled in that chair beside you?" I looked around immediately. I was surprised, but I understand he was overthinking and made no fuss about it. Unfortunately, your kid might have scarier pictures, and that is one possible reason he screams from his sleep or remains awake, scared to shut his eyes while everyone else was snoring off the day's works.

Teenagers are the largest class of extreme thinkers. They think they would grow up and become revolutionaries. They see the mistakes of their parents, and they feel matured than the youngsters, so they were sure they would make none of those mistakes. They dream of a perfect world where they grew and got an excellent job, family, became the celebrated boss and lived happily ever after. You can remember all of those infatuated dreams you had at teenage too. Those fantastic aspirations were always too perfect to be true. Of course, they looked genuine to you then. The problem now is that that big picture might make it hard for you to accept the reality. Everything might seem so different that you would think life was unfair to you, and you would rarely appreciate life. Every class of people has this problem, and it could lead anyone to overthink. Meaning, they would stare at you. But no, they were thinking of all the things they wanted, their fears, their failures, and doubts about the future.

Overthinking is actually complicated than that on other occasions. It is already becoming a problem that calls for urgent attention in far and wide of the world. It is a reason you would sit beside your best friend, and they won't hear you call their name until you tap them on the shoulder. The very wealthy people, the influential men and women, the single CEO at the helm of the company's affairs, and so on, they are all affected by overthinking. They'd sit in their big chair and stare so hard at the wall. You can tell better if you have been a secretary to one. You would stand before them and speak, assuming they heard you, but they heard nothing of your presentation because their brain was moving a mile a second in space. They were adding up other stats already. In their bed, the settee, at work, with their family, even in their dreams, they are always lost in their thinking world, and soon enough, their family and friends realize that apart from all of their problems, overthinking is one of the issues they have added.

Of course, you think very hard because you believe that is how best you could find solutions. That is about right, you can get answers by reflecting on the problem, but there is no reason you should sleep and wake up on the same problem. You will only expose yourself to psychological glitches. Have you tried to take a survey and see who could be overthinking around you? You would be surprised that your boss, your secretary, your spouse, and many more people are actually on this table, maybe, you too. I cannot overemphasize the danger of overthinking, and I hope that by now, a question would repeatedly pop in your head:

"How exactly can I stop getting lost in my thoughts and face reality for real?"

It is a big question. And it is one that I realize many people don't have answers too. Do you? You should close your eyes and think about that. If you are an addict to smoking, drinking, or chess, it will become evident to everyone soon enough, and you would know it yourself. But overthinking is a much stronger addiction.

Overthinking can make your confidence, your wealth, and your power get in your head also. You would suddenly begin to realize that someone was proud of you. Your spouse had no regard for you, your boss should respect you more, and your friends must begin to know you pay for their drinks and so give you that accolade you deserve. The thoughts in your head may seem simple to you, but you should remember Randolph Halliday saying that *"every human overthinks, and the moment they begin to behave according to their excessive thoughts, they would end in crises, rifts, protests, and breakdown in right relationship with others. They would also be filled with internal restlessness, if not pride.* Your excessive thoughts would make you wonder, 'what would Mr. Mike do to me if I showed up late at work? Nothing!" and then, you would begin to show up late. You undoubtedly understand what might happen after your boss labels you the infamous latecomer.

<u>Why should you know all of these?</u>

A lot of pictures should run in your mind now. You are starting to find what makes couples to nurture wrong ideas about each other. You realize why your best friend seems to be cold to you recently, and what prompts your favorite politicians to jaw wars. Authors sometimes bear wrong ideas about others, the same about scientists and even nations. I assume you can imagine how overthinking has a hand in world wars now, besides the fact that you now understand why a person may feel insecurity and pride without being directly attacked.

What is the way forward?

To bail themselves out of thinking disorder, many people result in reading on the internet as our research proves. Regrettably, they often read up cooked up articles and confusing pieces of information. A large percentage of people became more confused than they were, and fewer people got the proper drift after. But what happens to the others?

I have decided to compile this book to provide help to the larger masses who are overthinking. Whether they knew it or not. They will find the specific features of a person who overthinks in this book, so, from the first few pages, they can tell whether they are overthinking or not.

Gathered from vast research, solutions to overthinking are also listed and explained in this book. You will find out about the most significant cause of overthinking – mental clutter. I figured you would need to find out how to cure that, too, so detailed information is no doubt attached.

Apart from mental clutter and decluttering, I touched another issue that affects the human thinking; negative thinking, and of course, the solution; positive thinking. The world of the two topics is hiding some pages away from here.

You ever heard about meditation? Yeah, same meditation! It is one of the expressly discussed topics in this book. Why did I bother to touch that? Because the link between overthinking, positive thinking, negative thinking, and meditation is a thin line that can be cut off by nothing. You will testify to that yourself.

I shouldn't forget to remind you that I added good habits to the topic. It is one of the things you should have in your head right now. Your kids, your mom, your spouse, your staff, life would be easier if you have some good habits, and you could use them with your people. Sure thing, you can get them to learn once in a while too.

So, open your mind and get ready to learn the root of overthinking and the mystery behind it. Learn how to build a mental toughness that would help you remain firm and steer off overthinking and other problems mentioned. With this book in hand, you can improve your friends, families or colleagues who have these problems too. Hopefully, we could cure the world together if we go through the next few pages and use my advice, cheers to a carefree world!

Chapter 1: Overthinking

Let's take it from the top; what does overthinking mean? Overthinking is the habit of thinking beyond the necessary. It is the common habit of engaging yourself in constant thinking both at times that you need it and those times that thought would be a bad idea. You will artlessly do it when you cannot stop obsessing and worrying yourself about something. It is why you would sit at the canteen and play with the cutleries in the plate, rather than give the food a hungry bite.

The same thing that keeps you from picking any word from all those your friends were spilling around you. You would stare at the TV, but you would hear nothing of the loud disco bubbling from it. Your mind is so cluttered that if it was a room, we could say the files in it are littered like heaps of rubbish everywhere. You are always lost in thought, worrying about the future, regretting the past, struggling in your head to strike a balance in your to-do list, and wondering how to solve it all and turning your brain into a muddled mess.

Thinking is an excellent method of providing solutions. But you don't have to do too much of it to solve any problem. That is what most people do not understand. We all think so rigorously that everyone's head is cluttered with so many thoughts. And the fact that most people do not see it as a problem is what makes it more dangerous than most other addictions. If you are overthinking, there is a particular problem that is always coming into your head and taking all of your attention. For example, you may be troubled by the thoughts of getting your favorite car. Every time you think about other things, the thought of that car would always creep in. Let's say you are making a list of some items you need to buy at the mart, ideas of your desired car would suddenly pop in your head, and you would begin to feel reluctant about other things. 'Why should I buy this? I could add these funds to my savings for the car if I had a choice,' you would muse and fuss.

To make it brief, I am saying your world and thoughts would revolve around that car. It is the same with everything else that you desire. The lover you wish you had, or the house you would have loved to own. The power, control, or the position you want to attain at work. The amount of money you wish you control or the influence you are dying to have. Whatever you fancy too much can cause you to think less about anything else. Fair enough, the problem often gets solved when you get what you have always asked. It seems natural, right? Let's see this.

In some other cases, it is possible that you are not even thinking about a particular problem. It is all jumbled up in your head, and you have mental clutter. What's that? Mental clutter is a situation when many thoughts are jumbled in your head, and you cannot make out a straight one. You are vengeful about your dad who left the family or probably, the lover who walked away.

At that same moment, you are worried about the past that left some dark holes in your heart and the future that seems so uncertain and unpredictable. You need to get really better at work, or you would be thrown out sometime. You would continue to wonder what life has in stock for you; everything would seem so fogged. This type of overthinking is common than the initial one I talked about. Though, they both result in mental clutter, and the same person can suffer from the two types.

How do you know you are overthinking?

1. **You are always lost in thought:**

The first sign that anyone would observe in you and immediately guess you are overthinking is that you are forever lost in thought. You often find it hard to concentrate on anyone or anything. You would stand before your boss, and she would ask you, 'what did I say, Ms. Halyna?'. You would jerk out of your daydream and stare at her. You heard nothing of all she said. It is okay if this happens to you only once in a long while, but the instant it becomes incessant, you have a tough job to do on concentration.

I attended the gala of a young man in his thirties. He had just launched one of the biggest companies in the industry that year, and he had invited essential people to a celebration dinner. High ranking colleagues, families, and business partners were invited. I had been his father's counselor for a long time, and so his father's fax came that I had to be at the party too. Trust my strong merriment spirit. I ensured I was there. Everyone praised this young man and his initiatives at the party, and he laughed heartily at their jokes, but I thought something wasn't right about him.

Shortly after, his father drew me to a corner and explained that his son, the celebrant, was having a psychological problem that he wouldn't share with anyone. I frowned and left the man. I understand the assignment and got to it immediately. I studied the young man every time he spoke with people, and I saw what that troubles his dad about him. The young man was talking to everyone, but he could barely hear anything they said. He was not concentrating on what anyone was saying. He merely grinned now and then to hide his non-commitment.

I found his secretary and asked him if this man had always been this way and he told me, 'Sir, my boss isn't deaf or dumb, but I had to say to him the same thing over seven times. He already forgot as I said it, or he had no idea I was speaking at all. We all saw the glaring indication; he has a problem already, overthinking.

2.   You have more than three answers to a question.

One other way you can identify anyone who overthinks is that they provide ample answers to a single question. You could turn to your husband and ask, 'do you think snow might fall in January?'. If he says 'well it might because it did last year. It also might not because no rule says it has to, and even the weather scientists are not sure about its feasibility. Probably, it is too early to tell except if we have to dig the long books into deciphering whether it's been an annual or biannual thing…" Forget it, your husband overthinks. He has over a dozen answers already, not three. It is okay to be proficient in a topic, but you would likely not provide more than three solutions.

It doesn't matter whether they are casual, formal, or leisure talks. If you are always trying to provide a bunch of answers to each question you answer, even when the problem is not on your niche, you should note that you are beginning to overthink. Much more than the first sign we talked about, you can take note of this yourself.

3. You can tell how a situation inevitably ends:

Either you or some of your friends are pretty good at predicting the result of things. You are the type who knows exactly what would happen by the time the movie ends. You can predict who would win the basketball game or who would lose at hockey. By merely thinking about things, you can point out the plant that wouldn't survive the weather, and you often turn out to be right.

You are not different from anyone else in the room, but everyone will turn their head to you the instant someone asks a critical question that requires intense thinking. It may sound thrilling that you are telling them things they don't know, but you might be treading overthinking with this. According to Henry Bost, being able to predict results is a sign of a healthy brain, but if it becomes extreme, it is mainly because such a person is overthinking.

4.   Your instinct is saying too many things.

Our instinct is one of the most significant gifts of nature. Once in a while, you find yourself at the crossroad when you need to make an important choice, everything seems delicate, and you don't know what to opt for. The best method you can adopt at times like this is to look deep into your heart. Shut your eyes and let your heart speak. As it has been proven, our heart can provide a lot of solutions if we pay attention to it, especially in situations when you have no other option. Let's say you raised an Ad for a job and two men showed up. They are equally competent and you can't tell who exactly to hire. You may look into your heart and make your pick.

Your heart can tell when you are right or wrong. You can hear it whispering its choice into your head when you are about to make rash or critical decisions. The whisper would appear loud and unique, and you can't ever get it wrong if you listen to it. When you are considering investments, applications for loans, jobs, employment, and so on, what your heart whispers is as crucial as the facts you can gather. You could walk away from a million-dollar job because your heart feels something isn't right about it. You could also choose to start a mild life because your heart wants it, despite having a rich family background. In the end, you always find happiness because your heart had chosen it. All these are why everyone must hear their hearts out.

Unfortunately, you may be struggling to understand your own heart. You keep trying, but you can't seem to hear anything from it. Sometimes, you are sure it is telling you things, but they are probably too many at once, and they are getting rumpled in your head. The reason this may happen is that you overthink. You have forced your mind to generate more than one response every time, and that is why you get more than what you need. If you are the type who would not slow down sometimes and hear what your heart is whispering. Most likely, you believe you can think things through, you cared less what your heart says, and you have taught it to shut up. You would hear nothing from your heart at times like this. But if you are sure your mind is saying too many things at once, or it seems to say nothing at all, you should look out for other features of overthinking listed here, you are likely involved.

5. Deciding is a tough job

The inability to make a solid decision is another feature of people who overthink. You should study yourself more. Almost all the time, you find it challenging to start up and make decisions. You can see the harmful effects of all decisions even before taking them, and you cannot shut your eyes at them. The breakdown of all choices keeps running in your head and you sometimes, you had to call some of your friends or family to decide for you. A widespread example is investing in a business. You can see the risk and the profit at the same time, and you just don't feel sure you should venture into it.

For example, when Mike was still overthinking. He said he had just completed his high school and he wasn't sure where he should attend. So, he had to choose between proceeding to college or picking up a profession. While his friends had all made their decisions and visitors, he sat home for a long while, thinking about what best he should do. He wanted to be a professor, but being a professor might take ages. He could venture into the business world, but that would mean he has thrust a knife to his professorship dreams. In the end, he had to invite his family and friends who had always bailed him out.

6.　You repeat what you just said

Forgetfulness is another common feature of anyone who overthinks. You would find it hard to recollect what you have recently announced or what just happened. You would be surprised when you call your friend to tell him you would be out of town in a week and he replies 'hey bullhead, you said that to me just thirty minutes ago! 'really?' You would hang the call and keep asking yourself, "did I?". For some, they were having exciting talks a second before they picked the cellphone. Right after the call, you would have to remind them where they stopped what they were talking about.

I have a friend who would give a speech to the middle and forget what he had said. You have to remind him immediately lest you won't get the other half of the sentence, and that is not all, he could deny issuing the first sentence. It is okay if this happens when you are getting old. You don't seem to remember much, and you are always thinking about multiple things at a time. You would worry about your child, your vase, the dog, and so on.

But forgetfulness doesn't affect older adults alone. A lot of young men and women hardly remember what they were talking about before the secretary came in, and that is not near okay. They don't remember what has been bought, who has been paid, or when. Their secretary had to walk in and remind them now and then to guarantee they don't miss their appointment. It is so intense with some people that they would sit at a restaurant and order a meal, when you bring the meal as a waiter, they would stare at you, surprised. 'did I order a meal already?' The attendant had to start narrating how it happened all over.

7.   You are often anxious

A person who looks tense every time is definitely concerned. They keep looking around or stealing a look at other people's faces. They want to be able to tell if you approve of their work or you are pissed off. Of course, their head hangs lows when they talk to other people. They try to dodge everyone's face so the uncertainty on their own would not be exposed to others. You will find at least one person who does this if you work in a large staff office. Some people are actually calm and you would see them keeping their heads down, but a calm person would be quiet, not timid.

A nervous person is struggling with the condemnation they imagine in their head. They wonder if anyone would like them, if they did the job well enough, if their spoken language is excellent or if they won't get into trouble with someone. None of this is apparently worth losing sleep over, though; an anxious person still pictures all sorts of them in his mind.

8.   You are bad with deadlines

Being bad with deadlines is an unfortunate weakness of overthinking executives. For some reason known specific to them, they often believe they could hit the deadline and combine other activities together. For example, a director of the customer relations assures the board, "Gentlemen, I would deliver a presentation on a new customer relation strategy in two days, thanks." If this director gets engaged with many other tasks, she might find it hard to provide an infallible structure by her deadline, or she might even forget that deadline.

'ding!' she would nudge out of her thoughts the instant she remembers the headline, and she would try to concentrate on the job at hand. Unfortunately, she would soon remember something else and 'ouch!' she would divert her attention towards that too. All around, she would make efforts to strike a balance, and often times she would, with rigor.

You do not have to be an executive before facing a problem like this. Once you notice you hardly remember the deadlines you set for essential things in your life, you should begin to understand that some other factors are keeping you busy, and you are most probably overthinking.

9.   You sleep like a watchdog

Sounds harsh. But that is right, people who overthink usually sleep like a watchdog. They would roll about both sides of the bed, turning to each side every second, subconscious. They are definitely trying to catch some good sleep, but their overworking brain is not ready to spare them a chance. Remember I told you that they force their mind to think even when they are asleep. You do it by pressuring your brain to think about one sole problem all through the day. If this span into days and you still think about one ultimate issue, your brain would naturally pick it up, and you would find yourself thinking about the same problem when you quietly lay to sleep, or dreaming about it when you manage to. Too bad, nobody said dreams like that would be pleasant.

Anyone who overthinks does not always lose their sleep. But more often, they do. It is common with people who think about a particular problem. You may be worried about the dying child at the clinic, and it could be your lover who called for divorce, the career experiment that fails every time, and so on. They contact a health specialist, but all they get is a series of suggestions and a pack of pills that work only for a short time. The permanent cure they can apply is to stop thinking so hard or get themselves clear of that problem. But as you know, many don't even realize they are overthinking.

As you would soon discover, there are a lot of reasons people clutter their heads in overthinking. I will discuss them more in the next chapter. But for now, I would love to draw your attention to a part where you should raise concerns: most people who suffer overthinking don't get help. That sounds absurd, and it could tempt you to wonder: "really? Why don't they?" Let's talk about that.

Reasons people who overthink do not get help:

a. They don't believe they have a problem

It is easy to help someone when they understand that they need help. They would likely raise the cry for help themselves. It is what you would do when you wake to a sore down your throat or left ankle. But when you don't think anything is wrong with you, it will be difficult to convince you that there is something you need to work on. Can you remember that problem that everyone would point out to you, but you would jerk off and scream at them, 'I am fine!'. You probably may not be, but you certainly don't think you have a big problem at hand, and that may be the problem. *Del Pepal's Interns*, a counseling company in Spain reports that at least 45% of respondents in a 2017 research are overthinking, and they do not even know it.

When your best friend is always lost in thought or providing seven answers to one question, he is likely overthinking, but he may not even believe he has a problem and that would make it hard for him to think about solving the problems you saw. If you tell him to stop trying to think hard, he would give you an insolent look and ask you why. He would wonder if you had no idea that he got his solutions by thinking hard, or you don't want him to provide solutions to problems the way he does. You would probably think that way if you are in his shoes. You would refuse their suggestions and medications, and you would continue to live with that problem, which may get worse every day. Also, you definitely won't bring yourself to a counseling psychologist since you don't think you need one.

b. Nobody knows you have a problem

Sometimes, you are overthinking and you don't know anything about it. But if your friends and family notice this, they may set to help you by breaking your thoughts every time they see you are becoming immersed in it. Your husband would suddenly speak louder so you could hear 'hey baby, today is Friday!'. Words like that can jerk you out of your wonderland. You would find it hard to concentrate on thinking if they happen now and then.

But in a case that nobody thinks anything is wrong with you and you don't notice it yourself, there isn't much help coming for you. You naturally assume everything is fine and you would keep thinking that way. In fact, your friends, colleagues, and people who love you will encourage you to think harder about everything. 'What do you think, Joan?' the director would face you, 'I think we should give him some time' you might think hard and reply. 'What if he doesn't appear?' another member of the board might shoot at you, and inadvertently, you are coaxed to look in your head and find another solution again. You are definitely thinking hard, and you are growing prey to the dangers of overthinking. What are the risks? Look out for them in some of the following lines.

c. They didn't know what to do or who to see about it

In some other cases, a man would stand at his desk and ask himself, 'hi harry, don't you think we are taking things too fast, I think we might go insane if we continue to think so expansively.' I find it amusing that if you hang around and watch this man sit at his desk again, you would see him revert to his full-scale thinking. Thinking about his wife, his job, making calculations about his clients' demand, and how he would meet them et cetera.

A common problem people have is that they think beyond measures, they realize it, and they don't even know how to stop it. Thinking, and yes, overthinking is an unconscious action. You do not even know when you swing over your consciousness and got lost in your imaginations again.

d. They don't use the bits of opinion they got:

Finally, this is another reason a person who overthinks may still find no solution to his problems. It happens when they get a few opinions from friends and colleagues who have had similar problems. 'go to bed early, don't spend too much time alone' friends and families would casually say. But we have that friend who would hear us out, listen to all the suggestions everyone brings, and still do nothing about them.

Sometimes they do this because they don't believe there is a problem with them, and other times, they never considered the opinions. Soon enough, their friends and families would learn to shut their mouths and look away.

So. What leads one into the overthinking fit?

Chapter 2: Causes of Mental Clutter.

Do you remember Mental Clutter? I explained that it is the condition when too many thoughts are racing in your head. In the words of Ryan Nicodemus, who has worked on Mental Clutter his entire life: the voices screaming in your head won't stop. The project that needs to be delivered at work. The family basketball you promised you wouldn't miss again on Thursday. The drama your daughter got a role in, and she's promised not to forgive you if you don't show up. The promotional examinations you were writing on Saturday and the list continues to go wider.

Every one of these things is in your head. You have made some mistakes with your kid, at work, and so on, and you can't afford to blow any of the new changes you got now. That is precisely what we call mental clutter. You would struggle to concentrate on one, and another pops up in your brain like a computer mail notification. In fact, you would skip your meals to cover up some of these problems, miss your pastime with your family and still find yourself in the problem. What to do? Trust me, I will tell you.

But before that, you need to view a complete list of the causes of mental clutter. Of course, you now understand that mental clutter is what causes disordered and excessive thinking. You will soon understand how you got stuck with this problem in the next few lines. This way, you can tell if you or someone close is already overthinking, and you can go on to pick the most applicable from a list of solutions I will be providing after.

Causes of Mental Clutter

a. **You are scared of having no solution**

Being scared is okay. It leaves a tingle of excitement mixed with eagerness in you. But you have to keep your fear in check. That is what most single mothers, double-shift working parents, and people who have superiors worry about. They knew they had to be home for the kids, they needed to be at their schools, and at that same time, they had to work out a rocket science at their workplace.

Most of the times a client walked into my office and cried about making the wrong decision. I realize that what forces them into thinking out of width is *fear*. They needed to find a solution to their morass, and they hated the round of humiliation, sadness and rejection that would follow if they failed. 'How do I tell my ex I needed to work the night shift and I won't be there for the kids, he's warned me he might sue for full custody of my baby!'. 'Who would stay with my frail Pop if I don't turn down the dinner invitation from the man I love, and how do I tell him I am not going to make it? There is a ton of tasks at work too, what would happen if I don't get them done?'

Once you have more than one problem to deal with at once, there are very high chances that you would be obsessed with them and you would be worried about failure. You would scan all the tasks in your head furiously and worry about being unable to find a solution to each and all of them. But why pass yourself out on the problems and their chances of failure or success? It makes more sense to take the problems one after the other and draft a list of possible solutions for them. The costs of failure or getting no solution would ring in your head and heart.

b. **You are engaged in obsessive thinking about the problem**

This is an extension of the first problem I have shown you. I remember asking my secretary to stop working one evening. He had recently typed a paper and it was replete with grammatical errors. That wasn't like him, so I called him in, and we sat at coffee. We talked about basketball and I suddenly asked him, 'what is wrong, what are you worried about?'

'My wife wanted me to have a spectacular vacation with her in Australia,' he placed the teacup on the stool and focused. 'but I don't have enough, and I don't know how to get it.' I had to be home early because she was out of town and the kid is too young to make his way back home from school'. I looked at him and sipped my tea. I listened like an audio recorder as he poured out his mind, then I stood up and patted his shoulders. 'Mike, do you notice that in all you have said, you have mentioned the problems you have, but you haven't considered at least one way out of any of the problems.' I watched his eyebrows crease in realization, that was right.

From my empirical research records, up to 35% of respondents in Prince of Edward Island agreed that they had problems, and they were so worried about the problems that they didn't think about the solutions immediately. The problems were in bulk; thus, they practically forgot they could solve them one before the other. If you are the type who gets obsessed with problems rather than solutions, 'there are ten big problems to solve at home and at home, where do I begin?' will be your famous rhymes. You would keep reciting the problems and you may not be steady enough to sit and thrash one before the other. On the opposite, your igniting question could be 'where do I start, which can be solved first?'

c. **You believe overthinking solves the problem**
This is the most ironic fact of the whole story. Perhaps due to the famous quotes we all read at college, a lot of us believe that the real solution to a problem is obsessing your life with it. Think and think till you find a solution. That may be right; an idea might pop in your head if you keep making your head work on a problem. But that has limitations. Nobody spends their whole life thinking about a sole problem. If you find anyone like that, you should watch them; they don't go far in life.

A lot of scientists who made monumental discoveries did not focus on the discovery their whole life. Whatever discovery they made was a part of the large research work they were performing. So, there is no reason to sit at work, at the dining, in your bed, at the spa, at the cinema and still think about the same problem.

A client, Nicole, once asked me after I gave her a similar suggestion: if I don't think, how do I get fast and immediate solutions to the funds I owe, or do I have to declare bankruptcy?' I understood her and I smiled. She seems to believe thinking is the solution itself. She assumes if she thinks very hard, the solution would be in her grasp somehow. 'But what happens if there really isn't? Have you ever visited the psychiatry and met people who became patients for their wild imagination?'

Overthinking does not always solve the problem. If anything, it draws you away from your friends and families who might have better ideas if you mildly told them about the problem at dinner. If you can't trust their judgment, you should walk to a train station and talk to any random person at ease. You will be surprised that you could get meaning to life from something this simple.

d. **You do not see a counselor**
   This is an important part that too many people don't take seriously. Statistical analysis reveals that at least 65% of citizens of the United States would not book an appointment with a counselor until things were awfully out of hands. They believe they had tight schedules, and fixing an appointment with a counselor could only steal out of their time. But there is the fact you are missing, if that's what you think too. Counselors are like doctors. There is no perfection in the human body and soul, there is always causing you pain and worry in your heart, and there is still a health precaution you could use better. This is why one of your stable schedules must include seeing lifestyle and healthcare professionals.

If you maintain a stable schedule with your counselor, probably every fortnight or about, you could pile a list of things that take your time, activities that wear you out, problems you are worried about, and share them all with your counselors.

A professional counselor can also read people; she can tell when someone is depressed, scared or thinking. "hey, you are moving a mile a minute, what's the problem?" a professional could tell you how you are feeling or how much you have been tasking your head the moment you get into talks with one. That way, she can figure out the moments you are overthinking even if you had not told her, and trust me, you won't find it difficult to accept that from trained personnel. Right away, you would begin overthinking therapies too.

e. You are not paying attention to your health
How well do you consider your health? How often do you consider your health and wonder: is this really safe for me? If you had made it a full-time job to maintain good health, then there is a lot you wouldn't do now. You would practice simple workouts, healthy diets, no junks, timed break at work, et cetera. Believe me; you would practice moderateness in your thinking style too.

Let's say you are the guy who spends an extended part of his Saturdays in a basketball court, playing, clapping, and enjoying the thrill. There are Saturdays that things would get tight. That is probably because you have a lot more to do at work. So, you thought you'd better steal some time to get it solved on the weekend. You could go on and spend your weekend there. But trust me, your brain would not feel as relaxed as it often was on Saturdays. That may even affect the rest of the week. Now, you may be wondering, 'what should I have done then? If you ask me, you should risk playing what gives pleasure to your brain and watch yourself work like magic.

If you allow your brain enough rest, laugh, and have fun with whatever troubles you, an idea on how to solve it might suddenly drop in your head.
It is the same thing as eating. 'I can't wait for breakfast!' you would yell out to mom and jump into the taxi, your head already full of how you would resolve the day's problems. But that is absolutely wrong! Have you tried to compare how you work on an empty and how you do it when your stomach has had its fill? Don't even try to twist this; nobody works better on an empty belly! Whatever guarantee good health should not be toyed with, your thinking is healthier, more productive, and won't be shackled by hunger.

f. You are worried about the time

Time is another problem people worry about. Rather than focus on the problem and its solutions, about 52% of women in Pennsylvania who cannot handle pressure are always concerned about time. Right, time is a factor that drives one crazy, you can't pause, you can't stop it, you can't even shout 'wait a second!' and hope for anything. It keeps tickling towards the period the solution is expected.

The deadline for your enrolment and payment is a couple of days away. Your child's tuition is due. Your team has a big project that can turn everyone's face to your company. You are running out of time, and that alone is making you run crazy. You simply wish you could hit at something, someone, kick anything, and stop the whole madness! If there is more time, you could get one done and look forward to the other.

It isn't easier if you are just a staff member and the team leader keeps yelling at you to move a quadruple your speed and turnout something huge. You would keep staring at the time and your brain might start tickling the clock rather than the solution. This is why you must learn how to handle time pressure in cases like these. It is fine to check the time and see it tickling, but never should you let it tickle to the point of reflecting in your head and heart. Take your mind off it as soon as you can and focus on the problems at hand. I will tell you more about handling time pressure later.

g. You are getting emotional about the risks
This is one problem I hate to come across at work. It happens when you suddenly feel the pressure, the demand, and the urgency of the job in your body. The emotion climaxes in your brain and all you would love to do is get the solution anyhow. If you have to choose between taking a mortgage and renting a flat, you might opt for a poor choice because you had a rift with your spouse and you want yourself out of their house immediately. I once worked with a manufacturing company that had a high market demand at some point. It was unusual, so they began to pressure their staff to overwork themselves within the working hours. 'faster! Faster! Move it, everyone!' you would hear each

department manager scream at the top of their voice. It was crazy and the manager's reverberating voice pierced into everyone's veins.

Regrettably, a lot of the staff members didn't handle the pressure well. Many became emotionally pressured, and they made a hell of mistakes. Many typists mixed what they were writing with what they are thinking. The machine operators mixed the wrong proportion of ingredients, in the wrong order. It didn't take the managers long to realize that if this strategy would be used, many people would have to be thrown out or the company would run into a loss. Of course, the latter happened because the workers kept handling the pressure with a jumpy emotion.

At times like this, no counselor can do much for you because your brain and your body system are not relaxed enough to use anyone's suggestion. If you are the type who does this a lot, you would get home and begin to tell yourself by the mirror 'damn. I should have made three orders, not five'. You would sit at dinner and suddenly realized that if you hadn't been under pressure, you could have done something better. It is never okay to be under pressure, or worst, emotional disorder, and you must preach that to your body system every time you are about getting into one.

h. You have no definite plans, paperwork, and direction for yourself

Finally, we have to talk about you. What's your plan originally? To stay with Ma till you grow grey hairs? To leave for college and build your world there? To get married and never have a child? If you don't have a rigid plan from the start, you will keep getting into all sorts of problems. I will tell you that the first reason you were unsure whether to laugh or cry over your pregnancy was that you had no clear plans.

You would have known and prepared for it. It wouldn't have shocked you that someone is kicking you out of their house. You would also have been able to plan whether you would be going to see your daughter's drama, stopping at the dentist or meeting the crediting firm on Saturday. Having a concrete plan saves you a lot of stress, time and energy, assuredly.

Some people prefer to use the daily calendar, the phone reminder or the room alarm to keep themselves working toward the plan. That is not bad, but what should work better for you is your mind. Train it to remember your plans. Note them down and pin them on a table near, board, or wall near. You would find it much easier to cross or substitute anything when unexpected assignments appear. With that, you won't get into a fit of emotion, thinking, or plans disorder.

i. **You are demanding too much from yourself**
This is an amazing fact that many people do not even notice about themselves. We recently examined the staff of three large companies. We identified the people who think more than necessary from our survey, and we obliged them for an interview. From their responses, we realize that most people had tasked themselves to produce more than what their bodies could. They wanted a great life for themselves. They wanted to put a

smile on the faces of the people they love, and they wanted to get into the world on their own, free from other people's support.

These are all realistic dreams. But they are hemmed in a condition that makes it extremely hard for them to succeed, and as such, they would need the support they didn't want. They would get the high life they wanted but not at that spot, and they would require some time to achieve their dreams.

As a practical example, you would naturally overthink if you are always forcing yourself to think about the life you wanted but not getting. The cars you'd like to drive into your company someday. How you would love to try double shifts so you can earn more and show everyone you could do something. This is a very realistic dream. But you are against reality.

There is a limit to how much your body can be active if you work day and night shifts, and that is why you could breakdown soon, while you still mirror yourself as a massive failure. In another case, you close very late at work and still charged yourself to pick your son at school. You plan to spend some good hours working at home, and again return to work early in the morning. Tell me, how did you think this would work? You will only result in brooding if you keep setting unrealistic targets for yourself.

Have you discovered where you belong and what type of mental clutter affects you? Let's see how we can get you out of it.

Chapter 3: Declutter your Thoughts.

Just in the last few lines. I have shown you the world of a person with a cluttered mind how their minds could be occupied with so many things that are outside their control. When those things are within their control, they end up making off beam decisions. They result in overthinking and find it hard to concentrate on any of their problems. I have listed some causes of that too. Now, how do you help a friend, a relative, a staff, or yourself out of overthinking?

Techniques and strategies to declutter your thoughts

a. **Gear up your spirit**

Spill it to your spirit. It is time to move towards a saner and happier life. I have always maintained it. You can't do much if your body and soul aren't willing to go far with it. If all you need to do is get into a car and drive somewhere, it is easier to neglect the nagging voice in your head that insists on going nowhere.

But in a case where your soul decisions and implementation have to come from the mind, you dare not discard what your mind thinks. Let's take the case of a boss who loves a man in her team. She could keep thinking of him day and night, despite that she wanted to get him off her thoughts. No matter how she tried, there is no two-way out other than that she trains her mind to treat him as a business colleague and nothing more. In fact, everything else would make her love him more.

That is precisely how it works in matters of the mind. This mental clutter that resulted in overthinking is a matter of the heart. Your mind is becoming attached to so many things that it keeps returning them to your head, no matter how you try to concentrate on something else. It is like a heedless computer that keeps popping notification on an upgrade. Or that adamant secretary who returned the same file to your table every 30 minutes. To get out of the problem, get a firm resolution in your heart first, we are done with negativism!

b. **Begin with physical clutter**:
Now begin with physical clutter. I often repeat that physical or environmental clutter is as bad as mental clutter. What you hold in your head is a result of what you have around you sometimes. You will be held in a sour mood if you are always in a disorganized room, office, or environment in general. There is no way you can get yourself organized if you are still at a desk littered with poorly arranged files. This is why you must begin your struggle for a sane and stable brain with a stable environment. With a well-arranged stack of files and simple tools on your table, you can pick a file and restrain yourself from selecting any other file until you have treated one to satisfaction. Trust me; you can continue that way and handle all of the files without getting emotional outbursts in your head.

Naturally, the opposite would be the case if those files were littered all over your table. Your eyes would roam from one to the other, making it hard for your brain to settle on one and find tenable solutions to them all. So, using the earlier strategy, you can handle all the files in your head and be sure you would suffer no mental clutter. You can apply this same technique to your home, your laundry, and each of all the tasks you have to perform. You only have to remember, physical declutter is a path to mental declutter.

c. **Draft up a plan, a self-routine**
   Drafting up a plan is a vital assignment for every progressive person. From a simple schoolboy to a high ranking CEO. Everyone needs a clearly thought and scripted plan of your plans, goals, movements, with the period allocated to each of them.

   Some activities do not deserve to even be a source of concern, but having no plans for them might see them gradually becoming something to worry about. For example, 'what would I eat this morning?'. You will naturally assume something like that isn't a problem. But if you have two hours to prepare for work, you would unconsciously spend the first 15 minutes debating what to eat. In fact, you could grow a mental clutter and begin to grow a not-so-excited spirit from arguing about food. At the end, you end up eating nothing, and the loud grudges in your stomach would give you a really bad day.
   According to the popular lifestyle analyst Melita Esler, teenagers and early youths have a very big problem with dressing; 'which of the shoes should I use today?'. If you

have that problem, you would spend the next 20 minutes debating what to wear after haggling yourself about what to eat. Putting on an unsatisfactory dress can give you a very uncomfortable day. Your brain would alternate between the jobs at hand and how much you feel sore in the dress.

When go through all of these when you can simply set a daily routine for such activities. Check out what you have in stock and find a way to reflect them all in your planning. You should create an emergency backup too.

d. **Set Priorities**

Setting your priority is crucial to your success to your business world. In the words of the famous Zenith Brahdon, "If you set the priorities and they ring in your head all the time, it will be easier to achieve them, and you would achieve the supplementary tasks."

You should have observed that you found it pretty easier to pick the next thing to do when you make a list of priorities. What is the most important? Spending time with the dying old man, eating out with your spouse, preparing the team report the manager had requested. You decide! We all have varying priorities, and you would find it easier if your priorities are always stated from the start.

You should cross out the avoidable tasks out or move them to the foot of the table. This is going to help you avoid mental cluster to a very large extent, as long as you set your priorities correctly. Which of the cases needs to be treated first? What comes next? Try to draft a to-do list, that should help you enormously too.

e. **Use a Journal**

Using a journal is a piece of advice that I cannot over emphasize. As proven in empirical reports, using a journal makes it a thousand times easier to compute anything you have to. You can strike out what is no longer necessary or what's been solved already. You can point out what needs to be done in a special ink. You can jot tips that can help you resolve each of these problems as they occur to your head. That way, you won't have a jam-packed head with pieces of ideas that seem to fit nowhere because you can't easily pick out here they fit.

Using a journal helps you realized how much you have done on each of the tasks at hand; it helps you remember where you stopped and what exactly you were going to do next. That is not all; you can offload some of the burden into the book, which means you do not have memorize or rack your head for statistics. Using a journal helps you to outline the vital piece and complementary pieces too. Good enough, you don't need a large folder, a few leaflets that can be dropped in your shirt pockets can do the wonder.

f. **Don't hold on to everything**

One reason you may never get over things is if you hold on to them. You need to keep bygones as bygones and not worry so much about them. It is right that if we could turn back time, we will probably do somethings better. We will certainly right some wrongs too. But why linger in the past when nothing can change that? You got fired already; you need to look forward to better prospects and make sure you set things right when you get your new life. The old lady is dead; you really should not spend every day of your life mourning her. The kid is in coma, but you are not a doctor.

It is important to your life, to your goal, and to your success that you quit worrying about things that you cannot even change even when they matter a lot to you. You need all the focus you can garner. Try your best to quell the terrifying voices, pictures, and monuments that keep reminding you of a past you hate. You don't need a negative experience to keep disrupting the progressive ideas forming in your head. Let it go.

g. **Limit what you struggle with in your head**
Medically, there is almost no limit to what our heads can keep. But we might have problem recollecting information if we stuff it beyond necessary. The record explain that some people are exceptionally talented. They can remember data, data, and facts without mixing them up. But that that does not happen on average. Facts and figures get muddled in the brain too easily.

If you want a fully vibrant operational memory, you must make sure you are not saddling your head with more than the necessary assignments. It is okay to sharpen your brain with exercises. Keep track of a different events, details of a dozen transactions, scenes of some dates, and so on, but be sure you reduce this the instant you begin to mix facts in your head. Adding more than average would result in recollection problems. You might begin to mix up facts on some important information, and you could forget details about them. That may turn out not be fun, especially if you urgently need to remember something, and you had to rack your brain for it.

h. Dodge Multitasking

Multitasking is great, yeah? I bet your answer is a yes. You could calculate the funds, the taxation, and the interest rates of Company A's deals in your head. You may keep thinking about Mrs. Ruthann's transaction details at that same time. And none of this stops you from listing the things you need to get for your son after work. Soon enough, you would begin to mix your child's prices with the interest rates you are still calculating in your head, and you might shut your eyes hard. Struggling to retrieve the right file in your head and sort things, but the more you try, the messier it gets. Has this ever happened to you? It is one fearsome upshot of multitasking.

Multitasking is possible. But you cannot afford to do it every time. No human can effectively handle more than one problem at each given time. Instead, the end product will be what mental clutter. You would be thinking about everything and suddenly, it becomes bewildered. This can unsettle your self-confidence and start a bad day for you. And you must avoid that by paying attention to just one thing at a time in your head. Carry out only one task in each period too. You should never try to multitask when you need to provide urgent solutions, dodge it, and pay attention!

i. Create a Personal Time

No matter how neck deep you are in your daily tasks, the best way to get yourself out of problems is to create a personal time for yourself. It is okay to relax even when the whole world seems to be waiting at your office. Create a personal time for yourself, every day or week, whichever works better for you. At a time like this, you should be distant from your cellphone or the computer.

Instead, spend it all in your bedroom, see a movie, laugh, force yourself to forget everything waiting for you. Go to an opera, sing for yourself, sketch simple drawings, and laugh at yourself. Tell yourself the things that bother you and try to make sure you let them go. Spend time in the bathwater and think about nothing. These moments can help clear your head, regain your energy, and handle every pending issue with a renewed energy.

j. **Stay Healthy**
Staying healthy should be the first job of everyone. We all work to earn some dough, live a healthy life, and make ourselves and others happy. astoundingly, many give no regard for their health today. In order to earn the doughs, you get yourself up every day and night, overthinking and cluttering foggy goals and plans in your head; mental clutter. Mental clutter is a reason you may never lead a healthy life. You would sleep late, wake with a strained body and a foggy brain, you would skip breakfasts and forgot to laugh at anyone's joke. You already have enough going through your head, and you didn't even hear your kid sister talking to you. Mental Clutter may also spawn depression. You would find yourself lost in thought all the time and constantly struggle to transpose yourself between reality and the thoughts in your head.

These are early signs of an unhealthy body system, and you must take actions the moment everyone keeps saying they are the new traits they see in you. Retrace your steps. Force yourself to eat even when it seems to take all the time away. Feeding your body system can make it relaxed and nourished enough to give you the brilliance and energy to tackle the day's task. Without cluttering your head, you would be able to think straight about each problem. Plus, you won't hear your stomach grunt about hunger. Don't skip medications too. You can handle tasks more when you are healthier. Besides, you have to spend more time with your family and listen to their jokes. Laugh as much as you can and do everything that improves your healthiness. Play a game, try home workouts. Breathe in and out and pause to listen to your heartbeat. Don't forget to stand by the mirror and mock yourself.

k. Don't delay decisions on each case

Delaying decisions piles the problems you have on your table; you have to stop it in some way. The reason you have so many files on your desk now. So many mails to respond to, and so many decisions to make now is that you didn't make some earlier. You should have, and you must learn to do it now. Don't delay what you can get done immediately.

In facts, some mails require a 'yes' or 'no'. You could have decided if you would be taking the mortgage or auto loan earlier. You could have struck a fine deal with company ABC before a competitor appeared on the stage, and you could have asked your momma to stand in for you at your baby's convocation. Now it is all a mess. You have to decide on the mortgage and auto loan, you have to stand up to a fierce competition for company ABC's markets. You have to find a way to be at the child's convocation despite having a meeting outside the country because granny would never appear in impromptu occasions. Why are you holed up in a decision making spree like this? Because you didn't make some decisions when you could have. It would continue that way if you don't find a way to clear all of these mess and make sure you don't get into a complication like that again. How? Make timed decisions.

1. **Don't demand too much of yourself**
   This is something I should tell you about. It is okay to love your family. It is fine to worry about your parents and your beautiful little kids. They deserve a great family, a wealthy dad and you also deserve to be strikingly rich. But you cannot achieve it by demanding too much of yourself. Your body is humane, it gets tired, needs rest and stops when it cannot muster that strength to go farther.

   If you keep demanding too much of yourself, you would keep assuming you are a failure, you are an idiot, and you are not even making half the waves everyone else is. You wouldn't guess you are doing your very best. You would keep thinking about the horrible pasts, the bright but farfetched future and you will naturally fall into mental clutter. Why? you are demanding too much of yourself.

Falling into a mental clutter cannot solve the problem at hand. You need to stop demanding more than necessary from yourself. Your body is like any other person's. Motivate yourself, appreciate what you do and don't feel bad about what you can't. Trust me, you can get better that way.

m. **Use a counselor**

One convincing way of clearing your head is talking to a counselor. I remember telling you how ideal it is to book appointments with a counsellor before you can't hold the center again. Share things that clutter in your brain and hear the counsellor's suggestions. If you are not sure about using a professional counsellor, you could reach a confidant too, especially your spouse, old friend or parent whose advice has always reworked your thinking. You don't need a crowd, a valuable person or two is enough to share your problems. That way, you won't have to bear it all in your mind and suffer mental clutters, it is shared, and it can't become a chaos troubling anyone's head.

n. **Shun negativity**

Negativity is the biggest emotional problem we have to fight in the world today. It has led men, communities and nations to grooves of hopelessness, helplessness and frustration. I have dedicated a whole chapter to this talk, you will find it in some of the coming pages.

o. **Create a meditation period**

It is impossible to ask you not to think about things that matter to you. Therefore, I am going to wrap up this segment by hinting you that it is okay to think. It is fine to stop everything and think about the things that matter to you. Of course, this would be done at your quiet moments. Times when you won't have to attend to anyone or anything, preferably, at home, and certainly with a pen and your journal. You may even make a list of things you would like to think about and jot down the solutions you find as you think about them. You should make sure you are in a comfortable position and clear of interruption. Do this once in a while and you really may never have to suffer mental clutter and its effects.

Purposes of Mental Clutter

Why is it necessary for you to get yourself out of confusingly crazy pictures that mix up in your head?

a. To increase your happiness

According to the legendary thinker 'Aristotle', happiness is the highest success anyone can achieve. With happiness, it becomes comfortable to achieve everything else. In fact, only a few other things would still be considered important. With happiness and a good ambiance, it would never be hard to go on and solve each tasks of the day.

But if your mind had been filled with clutters. You seem to have too much troubles and you can't concentrate. There is your promotion, there is your parents, there is the bills, your kids, your spouse, everyone seems to be choking you. How do you concentrate? It is practically impossible. This is why you must make it a job to get yourself out of your mental clutter as soon as you can.

b. To burgeon your productivity

Have you imagined why people turn prolific at work? You would have two staff members perform the same job, but one will always perform faster, better and satisfactory when compared with the other. If you are wondering, "isn't that because one is adept at the job than the other?" You may be right. We are good at tasks better than each other. But in a situation when two people of equal expertise have been paired to do the job and one still performs better, what is the secret?

The mind. The commitment. The level of concentration. The rate at which they can get their mind to focus on the job at hand and not roam about other problems they have to solve. That is the difference. The level of mental clutter in your spirit can determine how productive you would be when you handle jobs. The synergy between jobs and concentration is so strong that the more you concentrate, the more you produce. Now, can you see why you need to find some way and clear off all mental clutters you feel in you?

c. To spread a positive energy

Positivism is what keeps the world rolling. It is the reason your staff, friends, and family would see you and blow smiles. They would tell jokes, give surprises and share in your excitement. It is also easier to handle problems when you are high spirited. You won't take it all up in your head to mental imbalance.

Phew, could you have missed the method to declutter your thoughts? Impossible.

Chapter 4: Create Good Habits.

I certainly told you about how having a steady schedule of some activities can save you from starting the day on a wrong foot. I did say you won't have to worry about what to eat or wear if you have them outlined on a schedule too. Remember? Great. Now, I am going to talk about something related, but bigger; Creating good habits. Naturally, habits form a big part of our lives. William James believes that at least 40% of what we do every day comes from the habit we have developed. The way we speak, think, wear dresses, smile, run, go about your jobs, go on and think of further examples, they are mostly from habits we have developed over a period of time. Smoking, walking and even sleep pattern or period are not exempted from this class. So now you get it, your habit is practically, the way you live. That is exactly why you need to create good habits.

Creating good habits is a pattern of behaving that can save you a lot of bucks. It is a way of designing your habits such that come what may, you remain organized, steady, in control and certainly out of mental clutter. Creating good habits has benefits that I would spare enough time to explain to you. But I have to let you know at this point. Creating good habits is a good idea, but it isn't a piece of cake. A lot of people start it and could not continue at some point. If you are in that category, you would find that most of friends will tell you 'This is what I am going to do." And you would mock them or wish them good luck because you think it is practically impossible to try what they were going to do. But guess what happens? They do it! Do you have an unbendable friend like that? They do not care about anyone's condemnation; they don't care whether it is easy or difficult. They just do exactly what they set out to do.

In your own case, you have a very different story. Whenever you set your mind on trying something new, you find it impossible to move far. No matter how simple or difficult the task is, you just never make a headway and you cannot explain why. You have tried different tricks and some of them worked, you were able to start the goals you set with them, thus far, you barely cover a few percent of the task before you lose interest.

I am proud to tell you that I understand what you feel at that moment. I also understand that if that habit is not conquered, it might become really hard, if not impossible for you to create good habits and include them in your lifestyle. I am going to end my declaration by announcing to you that it is okay to feel that way once in a while, as long as you don't let a feeling like that get into your head. Also, there are fail-safe remedies to help you out of that problem. There are simple steps that you should follow whenever you design to pick up a new habit and it is not working. I will show you how you can apply these steps in creating good habits, and you can go to apply them in other instances. Ready to see them? pop!

Steps to create good habits

a. Your mindset
I'd like to tell you again that your mind is the root of all problems. Your beliefs, ideas, and your reactions to

issues are all caused by all your mindset. The root reason you can't achieve those things at this point is that you are afraid of your old failure. You figured you would probably fail again and you are afraid that you are not up to the task.

Even when you try to stand up to it, you know pretty well that something in your heart isn't giving you its supports and so, you might fail again. Think about these last lines. Is there a fallacy in one? That is exactly why you have to battle that mindset from now. Before you can hope to create new habits, create a positive mindset. Your mind needs to agree that you could create new habits and wipe off all of your old habits, retaining only the good ones.

b. Write off competition

Keep in mind every time that this isn't going to be a competition with anyone. You are getting up and changing all of these habits by yourself and for yourself. No other goals. You would find it more demanding to compete with yourself and your set goals than to compete with anyone. If you must challenge your friends to a new lifestyle, let it be for the fun of it, not the competition, and don't make the competition your priority. When challenged to a competition by anyone, you should ask yourself before taking it up "won't this get into my head? Am I in because I want to get better than the or I simply desire to make myself better? Won't I ever guess jealous of them?" if you can find positive solutions to these questions from the start, solving the problem becomes a piece of cake.

c. **Start Small**

There is always a lot to do. There is always an empire of good habits to cultivate. You found something on a scholar's profile and you would love to emulate it, you found another in a famous book you read. You will definitely find a lot of habits you want to pick. But you must understand that starting small is juicy. It gives you a firm foundation. It lets you start at a range you can handle and go on to build a wider network. Do not worry about how much your friends are achieving or how fast you would like to learn and assimilate the behaviors, start small!

d. **Build consistence**

This is exactly where you have work to do. You cannot build a habit without consistence. You want to use the bathroom every night, do it without minding how tired you were you dragged in from work. You may challenge yourself with simple incentives or even heavy fines. For example, you could keep a candy, chocolate or your favorite snack in the tray for yourself. It can be taken only if you hit your daily target.

Besides that, you may stake a bet with friends, ask your spouse or mom to fine you every time you refuse to carry out the practice. You could also fill your room with motivational quotes of people who never gave up. One of those tricks would force you to continue.

"Damn, I can't give up" you would begin to feel the moment you step in your room and sight stickers of your favorite heroes who never gave up. You may also remember that your mom or spouse would nag like hell if you refuse to pay her the fine, so, you'd better get the task done and avoid the levy.

e. Set small goals within your primary goal: A pleasant idea you may try is to break down your goals. You want to be extremely good at surfing, go on and set targets for yourself. This week, you would learn about the board and standing on it. You planned to learn on a Tuesday and practice that all through the weekend before taking on anything again. Consistently practicing this can help you to master that step before moving on to the next step. Ordinarily, you could have learnt it all without mastering each phase, which means you could get confused at some point and get them wrong. But because you broke the main goal into simpler goals, it becomes easier to understand and proceed to bigger ones. You should learn to compensate yourself for every achievement too. You should try to apply this to other habits too.

f. Do it without thinking: The moment you stop thinking about practicing, it becomes a piece of cake. How do I mean? If you turn practice to a non-negotiable habit, it will become a strong exercise that you don't even want to break away from. If I was learning how to ski and my training were fixed for Thursday mornings, I would cross out every other activity at that period. I would consider that period my hallowed time and as such, it is not even part of the periods I could think about adjusting. If you can create a period like this to learn a new habit, you would learn it quickly.

g. Buy enough support: I completely recommend you do this. Learning a new skill or habit can be frustrating. Especially if you are growing old or you are too busy to spare enough time. Everyone around keeps thinking it is a waste of time and you need not work yourself out that much. This is why you should have a fans club. A couple of people around who think "yeah, it's a great idea, go on". They will remind you when you are getting too busy to practice and their encouragement is enough to get you back on track. Of course you don't have to put your support in anyone's head or heart, it is only that there is always someone who loves your idea and it is your job to find them.

Habits you may take up to declutter your mind

Now that we have discussed the methods you can adopt to make sure that you completely absorb a new habit. Let's talk about the habits themselves. What kind of habit should you consider adopting?

a. **Healthy diet, constant drinking and creative cooking**
this is one habit that can keep you in a dreamy land forever. Imagine returning from work with a very sour mood. But you stepped in the door and the mesmerizing aroma of a delicately made food hits your nose. Trust me, it will fill your senses and for a second you would be forced to erase the days' snag from your brain. You would look around and whatever plans you have made earlier would hang. You were probably planning to go straight for a shower, but now, your mouth must be showered with this yummy food. If you take up a habit like this, you would be dunked into it so much that the flavors would be the only drifting in your head, no mental clutter. Not just you, your friends, families and housemates would certainly share in your spirit.

b. **Controlling your words and manners with everyone**

This is another habit you must be aware of. How do people feel after you spoke with them? Like a piece of old thrash or an amenable fellow who could do better with suggestions from their superior? How people, especially those who are inferior to you feel after you have just addressed matters a whole heap. It is a good habit that can indirectly contribute to your rest of mind among others. It can determine how settled your mind is to attend to other issues and persons. If just to maintain your composure so you can handle all the problems you have, it is ideal to let things slide and not get mad at your inferior every time. Allow them a benefit of doubt, don't take it out on them. People naturally learn faster when corrected with respect to their personality, and trust me, you can do it.

c. **Drafting a workable schedule**

I cannot overstress how important this is for everybody. 'I wish I can be so organized!' you would hear a man condemn himself in anger. But hardly would he ever take any steps towards that. Ideally, being organized begins with having a plan. A proper schedule of how you think things would be workable. You can do this by making a reflective study of things you need to do in the coming day or week. Fix them in a timetable and remember to add the duration of each of them. You should consider bunging up the timetable so well that the time is well spent. Once in a while, allocate a free time for emergencies.

d. Allocating a personal time in your schedule

Among other periods that must be reflected in your timetable, personal time is a must. It is a superb idea to make out time for yourself. This period will be spent resting and reflecting. You could curl up in your bed or bath tub, lay your nerves and shut your eyes. Then begin to think of your interactions with everyone.

What was the look on your secretary's face? What was the reaction of your boss? Could you have done something better for your child that night? Should you have chosen mortgage over auto loan? This is the reflection hour. Think about it and criticize yourself as much as possible, but make sure you remember that some things cannot be changed and there is no point in making a fuss about them. It's in the past already, the only correction that would be made to them is to forestall anything like them again.

e. Cleanliness

Cleanliness and orderliness are brothers. There isn't much sense in organizing a pack of litters all around your lounge. Make it a duty to clean yourself and your environment. Your dress, teeth, hair, shoes and so on must be kept clean and neat. The most important is your heart. Don't fill it with thoughts of harm and hatred for others, neither should you occupy it with assorted thoughts of complicated problems. By the same token, give your environment your best shot in cleaning. Your files, your drawers, the trays, the cups, they all deserve to sparkle at all time.

f. **Timed decisions**
   Making timed decisions is crucial to the success of your organization. It is not necessary to respond to every mails immediately. You should not fight back every bout immediately. Sometimes, it is okay to stop and wait for the right moments. That is time consciousness too. But you must commit to your memory that some decisions are best taken immediately. They would only lead to further complications when delayed.

   For example, making a decision between staying with your kids or travelling for the business trip at night. If you remain undecided for too long, you might realize you have spent too much period thinking about it, and you could have spent that time on something productive. Now, your kids would be in bed by the time you return and you didn't obtain a ticket at the airport which means moving out is highly unlikely. Why not simply decide earlier and take the right steps?

g. **Sharing others' problems**
   I will continually encourage you to listen to other people. Have listening ears. Even when you get tired of listening easily, find a way to make the speakers take the bull by the horn and get the basics. You will succeed more as a leader if you learn to listen to the problems, ideas and suggestions of your followers. Of course, you are not obliged to follow them all, but you will surely know better if you listen to them. Study them, your friends and families want you to listen to them too. In the same vein, people are always willing to you, so there is no genuine reason you cannot share your worries with others occasionally.

h. Avoid intimidation

The golden rule of human states that you should do unto others only that which you want to be done to you. Familiar with that rule? You have to use it now than ever. You should remember that humans are only created to hold different positions, they are equal. Of course, you remain superior at work if the tables don't turn, but on average, you could treat everyone equally without a smear or disrespect on your image.

i. Patience

Patience is a good habit that can win you medals and nothing less. Keeping it cool with everyone is a way to keep your nerves. If you ensure you are always patient in every case, you will hardly get worked up over anything, and you would be meticulous enough to make the proper choices only. This is a prominent reason you should consider being patient at all times.

j. Hold sway on your emotion

Fair warning, you will come under pressure a lot of times. If you work in a customer relations or production unit, you already have some good idea what I am talking about. Your clients can be demanding to a point that you could almost lose your cool with them. You would get irritated by some requests and you might have to keep apologizing without getting angry in turn. It is hard to maintain your cool in cases like this, and that is why you must learn that habit.

In the wide world, we can metaphorically state that we all work in the customer relations, and everyone who walks up to us is our customer. They want to share ideas, information, and their disagreements with us. We must be able to keep our anger at bay when dealing with them all. No matter how offending their comments had been. This is a good habit that can save you from suffering a mental turmoil and at the same time, maintain a fair relation with the speakers.

k. Have a positive mindset

Having a positive mindset is a cure to many problems in the world today. Regrettably, positive mindset is exactly what more than half of the world does not have. It is what leads anyone to frustration, anger, impatience and finally suicide. Not having a positive mindset means you may never see the positive side of any action, decision or opinion anyone raises around you. You are solely concerned about the negative sides. But where does that get anyone? You will see progressive solutions rather than problems if you begin to use a positive mindset.

l. Setting a goal and working to it

This habit definitely belongs somewhere at the top. It is one of the first few habits anyone should cultivate. Setting a goal is crucial to having a direction in life. It determines your schedule, your friends, your enemies, your diets and so many other habits. You can only become successful if you have a goal you are working towards and you take on other habits as your progress in pursuit of your goals. Set your goals and work hard to achieve them. You can do that without becoming mental cluttered, especially if you get engrossed in some other activities.

m.   Relaxing

If you are someone who feels it is okay to overburden yourself because that is how you are inspired to do better, I hate to tell you that you are wide of the mark. You do not have to overburden yourself in order to achieve, you must learn to spare some time for leisure. If you are at some critical point that requires you to overwork however, be sure you compensate yourself afterwards. You should try to break out of the suits and ties for a pajamas or bikini. Find a way to relax your tense muscles and stressed brain. You need whatever could distract you from work for a while. You might go sun bathing, sightseeing, or stop at the cinema. We all have our different ways of relaxing, you should realize and don't wear yourself out before you use it.

n. Increasing your core values

On an encompassing note, another habit you can look forward to creating is maintenance. You are certainly not an entirely bad soul. There are a couple of habits that are good about you originally, you will also pick many here and begin to inculcate them in bits, but inculcation is not enough, you must find a certain way to preach them and instill them into your life stream permanently. There we are! The ways to create good habits and the most important habits that you can create; all at your fingertips. Let's go to the other side!

Chapter 5: Remove Negative Thoughts.

Furthest from what we were talking about only a page ago, negative thoughts are not what anyone should build. Negative thoughts are bad feelings and idea that sink into your heart and linger there. They would sit in a dangerous place in your heart, and make you see the negative side of everything. "Why should I support him?' you could hear yourself thinking as you listen to a gentleman who has just presented his business plan to him. "Why should I trust her?" You don't seem to feel like trusting anyone. "Is she the only one who has the right to success?" Envy comes with negative thinking too. "What if I run into a car and crush myself? What happens if he hits his head on his vase at his front?" All of those are pure negativism.

From the experience of Steve Bloom, he explains that these thoughts fill your head and make it hard for you to see the positive side of anything. Negative thoughts are what creeps in your head and cause to envy your best friend. You could feel anger at other people's success. You would entertain fear and doubts about everyone who cares about you. You will never be sure you should take risks, invest or take on a new adventure because your head is crammed with thoughts about the danger, harms and disasters that could result from these adventures.

You cannot continue to nurse thoughts like this. They would fill your head with mental clutters, overthinking and you would hardly be inspired to find a way forward in those situation. You would hardly be happy about anything. You don't think there is a solution anywhere and you get overly angry about anything. If you continue in a low-spirited mindset like this, you would hardly create good habits, and therefore, there is no progress in your career or development. If you ask me, you need to get rid of your negativism before you can look to build meaningful relationship with others in your world. How can you do that? I am going to put that in plain words soon, but first, what is the root of negative thinking?

Sources of Negative Thoughts:

a. Your past or present experience: In most cases, the reason anyone nurture a negative thought is that they are have a dreadful life. If nothing makes sense to you, you keep losing contracts and your ex-spouse keep pulling for sole custody of the kid, it will be hard to survive. It is worse if you can't find anyone to talk to. At times, it is because you have gone through some hurtful periods that no one seems to care about or understand. These past or present experiences may haunt you. They may lead to depression and they could look meaningless to you. You don't want to trust anyone and you fear taking on a new adventure.

b. Illness and drug reactions: Illness doesn't always cause pessimism. But at those times that you feel agonizing pains all over your body, you could become hopeless about everything. 'Nah, I am not going to survive this'.

You would doubt the power of love, patience, freedom and so on. You simply want to be dead. It is also possible that you begin to nurture negative thoughts and hallucination as your body's reaction to certain drugs. All drugs can't work for you, and so, taking some lead to counter reactions from your body.

c. Wildness: Humans have a wild mind by default. We have a mind that can roam into the highest points of imagination you can't believe. There are loads of thoughts that we cannot bring to reality, but our mind can imagine all of them in the twinkle of an eye. It would imagine the positive side and immediately switch to the negative sides. Your mind would be filled with 'what if and what if' so much that crazy ideas may begin to pop in your head from that. For instance, you saw a cute little girl and you might wonder, 'what if she is deaf and dumb? What if she is a terrorist's child? What if she is a human bomb?' zany ideas!

d. Cortisol: From the scientific perspective, John Brandon explains that there is a chemical in the human brain that causes negative thinking and depression. It is called Cortisol. It flows easily in the brain and it can be triggered with the slightest stimulant. For example, if I walk up to you and tell you 'do you know someone is talking thrash about you in the office?' Your brain would release cortisol immediately. You could become apprehensive and flame out "who the hell could that be?" That's it. Cortisol. "A truck fell at the market" I could tell you and the first thought in your head would be 'how many people died or what and what got damaged?' this is unquestionably, the function of cortisol. It is quicker to think about the negatives in each situation than the positive. A chemical that tries to oppose and reduce the effects of cortisol in the body is dopamine. You can only release more dopamine by forcing yourself to withdraw from negativity.

Now, how should you resolve your negativism?

a. Cut your thoughts shut: The first way to combat negativism is to cut it short. The instant it appears in your head, cut it off and try not to think about it. Take a crack at other thoughts and wipe your negative thoughts with them immediately. For example, you are about to endorse some investments funds and your negative thoughts suddenly pops "this might end in tears, you might…" cut it off immediately! Think about the food you ate; the football game you saw or any fascinating case that can fill your thoughts and wipe negative off your mind. Can you remember anything like that right now?

b. Query your thoughts: Negative thought is hardly trivial. It has a strong tone and presence that makes it extremely hard to discard. Due to this, you might have trouble crossing out these thoughts and you have no choice but to stand up to it. Now that you have to pitch a defense before this negative thought and launch your counter response, what do you do? Analysis. Do not analyze the circumstance, analyze the negative thoughts.

For example, I am about to turn on the power control on a machine and I suddenly wonder, 'what if the machine sparks?' I may try to brush that off but the thoughts may continue to linger: 'what is your way out if it is just you among all of these machines and the fire emanates from an angle of the room?'. Now, I know it is a serious business and I have to find an answer soon, else, it may become a thought that would fill my head all day or every time I walk into the engine room. I could then ask, "okay, what is the benefit of this thought? How does it make things better for anyone? I mean, how exactly does it help anyone?". Trust me, your negative questions would withdraw into the dark at that moment.

c. Ridicule your negativism and think of the worst: Has your negativism showed up? Fine, let's join in the banter. The worst treatment your negative thoughts wanted was banter. It wanted you to treat it with all seriousness. But it would vanish the moment you ridicule it. Let's say you are in that same engine room and a negative thought appears 'what if fire appears from one angle in the room?'. You can stop what you were doing and allow your mind to fully concentrate on a response.

Well, then another fire might shoot from that angle, one from this angle and the last one from the fourth angle. Then it would be just me and the engines and the fire would start catching the engines as it thins the space between us. Then I would jump up, I would shout and run up and down here. I would wait till the fire gets to me and begins to hurt me and burn my skin. I would run here and then like an insane man and jump straight at the door. Everyone else would have heard my noise and they would be waiting with a pump or bucket of water in hand. The instant I break through the door, they would shoot me with their pumps of water till I am filled with water again, instead of fire. They would then haul me in a van and straight to the clinic. My Lady Crush would then visit me and stay by my bed, she would tell me not to die and I would pretend...

Imagine! You have turned your negative thoughts to a joke! It has become so useless that rather than be scared of it, you turned it to an episodic drama you are enjoying in your head. That is exactly how negative thoughts should be treated, and you could use this as a direct substitute to the thought querying technique.

d. Explore the world: one other way to get yourself out of negative thinking is to explore the universe. Check out fascinating places. Visit as much as you can. Meet new friends. Ask people about them. Laugh at jokes people crack around you. You can live an entirely different life if you keep exploring the world. You would rarely remember whatever you were worried about as you got lost in the charms of a new community and its surprises. You could also go on a regular leisure walk. It would help you see new communities and lose your thoughts in the beauty of nature.

e. Look at the other side: Viewing things from another perspective can help you fight the disparaging talks of a negative thoughts. Rather than wallow in the thoughts and its negativism, you may simply choose to view things from the positive end. You are driving on a wide road and a zebra crossing lay at the front, for instance. You can see people walking across the lines and you had to wait till they are all gone. While you are waiting, a negative thought may suddenly whisper in your head 'I should crush these idiots. I could be 5 miles away if they are not here now, they are wasting my time!'. If you choose the *cut it short* technique, you would definitely try to stop from going any further in your head. But if that doesn't work? You might query your thoughts with questions or ridicule your negativism. If you are not so inspired to try any of those, you may simply try *the other side* technique. How does it work? Rather than think about the negatives, think about the direct positives. "what if I was in that position? How would they feel when they realize that the system recognizes them and plans their movement on the roads too? what if I had sped faster and run into some casualty?" This is how much your brain can do, and soon enough, your negative thoughts would thin out.

f. **Expect the worst sometimes**: I have spoken so much about the need to wipe out negativism in your thinking. I have even mentioned some techniques you can adopt to aid that. I will surely tell you more but I have to let you know at this point, it isn't such a bad idea to have negative thoughts. Once in a while in fact, you must seek your negative opinions on certain issues. Famous billionaires have reported that before staking a risk on any business or investment, the first factors they consider include the dangers of the initiative.
Could it fail? What are the chances of failure? What are the worst scenarios that could happen? You must learn to adequately prepare for all of these if you don't want to be caught by surprise. This isn't just for business; it happens in virtually all business related fields. So, it is

safe to think about the negative side sometimes, as long as you don't wallow in it, and you are using it for constructive criticism of the whole idea. This means if you must think about the negative sides of something, you have to do it moderately.

g. Use a lot of Affirmation: Affirmation are simple declarations. They are declarations you confidently make to yourself or others about a situation. They are useful both at times you know how to handle issues and times when you don't. Let's return to our engine room. If the thought of fire outbreak pops in your head, you might give it a shove by using a positive affirmation like 'nothing is going to happen in this room'. You may even say it out. Of course, there is no reason a fire should spark, but you have to crush that thought out immediately, so it doesn't haunt you or repeat in your head. If a fire actually breaks out. you may be filled with gory thoughts of death and pains, but you can use this same technique to keep yourself confident that 'nothing is going to happen to me. I am going to be fine. I am going to be alive!' though you are likely scared and unsure about what is going to happen, using affirmation can build your confidence. Affirmation doesn't guarantee that no hazard will happen, but it keeps you confident and it clears your mind off all sorts of negativity.

h. A journal you the rescue: Writing is an indirect of telling someone what you feel. You can think of how relaxed your heart feels after you have shared your problems with someone. This time, this *someone* would not even criticize you or expose your secrets to anyone unless you lead them to it. So, surely this is your best medium of expressing your worries out. Remarkably, empirical studies have shown that sharing a negative thought can reduce its potency on you. this means the moment you decide and share some of your worries to anyone, you have conquered some of your worst nightmares.

Ting-a-ling! So many alternatives. You can choose anyone you feel would work for you and get to it. Remember that you have to snuff out your negative behaviors before you could work towards positive thoughts. You should begin by identifying the exact source of your negativism and then the solutions. Which works best for you?

Chapter 6: Positive Thinking.

Positive thinking is one of the most powerful clauses you can ever come across. Undeniably, it doesn't seem to hold much value when you hear it. You cannot even compare it to bigger and wider terms like competence, competence, tenacity and so on. It seems really soft and fluffy in comparison. But it is much more than all of those concepts merged. While defining positive thinking, Remez Sasson says it is a mental and emotional attitude that focuses on the right side of life and expects positive results. Apparently, it is much more than having good thoughts and smiling every time. It is about creating real values in the life of others, by holding on to only the silver linings in your own life. Positive thinking helps you to go through your daily experiences with a mindset that handles all parts of life without making a fuss or lamenting about parts that didn't go as planned. It assists you to find happiness, joy, and progress in everything you do.

It is a kind of mentality that would keep you from fleeing the instant you look up and find a tiger waiting to tear you up. Knowing that you cannot run faster than a tiger, negative thinking would make you believe if you wait a second more, that tiger would pounce on you and devour you. But positive thinking keeps you in the game. It reminds you that running is a short-lived escape option, so you'd have to find better option. That could include dodging the tiger's attack, getting a club and hitting it or running up a tree. Within that space of time, your mindset leads you to find the nearest solutions available and use them judiciously. Seeing setbacks as ordinary games is the beauty of positive thinking.

Relatively, you may not come across a lion these days, but in the exact way a negatively thinking character and a positive thinking character have handled the encounter with the lion, a negative thinking person would hardly be patient in the face of pressure, emergencies or danger. But a positively thinking person can be trusted to handle the case better.

Kendra Cherry discovered that thinking positively can influence the growth and development of a human to a large extent. For example, a child who thinks positively would smile at everyone. She would run about the garden and hit football with everyone else. She would listen to your jokes, contribute and give questions when she was confused. She would not even mind that anyone was jesting her inability to pronounce the language correctly. This is the essence of positive thinking. You realize there are problems but you are not cowed by them, instead, you enjoy whatever happens.

Similarly, James Clear declares that an adult who uses positive thinking would age slower than anyone who doesn't. This is something you could have experienced if you have a grandpa and grandma, and you stayed around long enough to study them. It never mattered who was older, whoever laughed more, gave little regard to problems and never made a fuss about anything between them is always healthier. If it was grandpa, he might be older than his wife, but he would likely look healthier and full of life. If it was the wife, she would definitely add those features with beauty too. You would hear the animated person say to the other; 'oh yeah, I have old bones but I am jogging with all of them right now, want to come along?', 'no way'. As you would guess, the other person is forced to laugh and turn down the offer.

How exactly does positive thinking works?

There are dynamic traits of positive thinking that you can look out for in the life of people. These charismas or characteristics are not hard to find because they help the individual stand out among any group. You can build a lovelier life by imitating them and imbibing them as good habits, as much as you can. Remember we already discussed how to imbibed good habits into yourself, here we go. The next few lines contains a list of the basic features of positive. Check out those you have, and as for those you don't, I dare say you already know what to do, fire up!

a. **Daring to try something new**: Positive thinking makes it easy for you to try a new experience. It makes you confident in the face of uncertainties so much that you do not worry about what the outcome would seem, you simply go and try what you felt like. If you are the director of a company with large investments, you would be able to summon all the confidence you need to change your production style or invest in a new product, even at the detriment of your current production. You know there are risks of setbacks, but you would go all out in your investments basically because you believe in it.

You would likely do something similar if you are a staff member. You understand you earn a good dough at the end of the month, but you would be positive enough to muster your nerves and break away from the company. Probably to start your own industry or lookout for a better or much more comfortable alternative. Positive thinking is what gives a student the courage to change his area of specialization, after all, a lot of other students realize they were not comfortable with their current course of study, but they were worried about the rigor of re-enrolment and the fear that they may never adjust. So, they kept mum and remain unhappy with their course of study. In some other cases, you could pick your car and leave your family home in Santa Clara, off to Colorado where you don't even know anyone, but you have the guts to try.

b. **Hopefulness**: Hope is the strongest feeling manifested by positive thinking. Positive thinkers are prone to failure like every other person, but they have an enviable optimism that wouldn't let them give up when they can still win. They dare steps nobody expects them to win, yet, they perform remarkably than you would expect them to. 'I didn't realize I was doing so much till the university invited me for an award, Baxson Grey a computer science graduate of Wimbledon told the press at his award night.

A student who dumped his admission in Medicine to join a music school had pulled all strings of confidence and optimism. He had just showed the world that he believed in himself and he is not afraid to restart. He is completely hopeful and he looks forward to what lays ahead in life, in good faith. It is what happens when a peasant builds the balls to apply for much wider or bigger programs that they originally may not be considered for, but they would remain hopeful and look forward to favorable responses. Whether they got it or not, they remain unrepentant optimists.

Hope is not hard to read in the life of a positively thinking child. She would run after her brother to get her favorite candy from him. She would lift the basketball and keep trying to score, of course, she won't and she would not give up for frustration, she could only get tired. If you actually got yourself trapped in an engine room going up in flames, you would naturally believe it is all over if you are a pessimist. But as a positive thinker, you understand you are in trouble but you wouldn't worry about it excessively. You would rather focus and patiently wait for the perfect opportunity to take a survival chance.

c. **See good in others**: A positively thinking person would naturally believe in other people. They understand that life is not a bed of roses and so, humans are subject to troubles once in a while. If you are a positive thinker, it will be naturally easy for you to celebrate another person's success, even when you had competed for this same thing. They won't hold it on you that they lost, they would only celebrate your victory. A positive thinker believes that if a human is placed in a better condition, they would naturally perform better. This is why your positively thinking boss may begin to work towards salary increment for everyone and better terms of service. He would formulate theories about your lateness and assume you couldn't have decided to appear late to work deliberately, so, he tells you off most of the time. This doesn't make him a weakling in spite of this, he can tell when you hold a little regard for their job or you deliberately slacken your commitment.

When you did a marvelous job, expect it from your boss the instant he realizes what you did, positive minded people like to appreciate others. In the case that things go wrong, a pessimist chooses to assume that what went wrong was the fault of no other person except herself, but a positively thinking person believes it is no one's faults. If we are talking about you or your best friend, you will notice she would never blame herself or anyone else over her mom's accident, her dismissal and so on, she would simply move on. Great experiences should be celebrated by everyone, and the bad ones, well, no one deserves them, and they shouldn't be attributed to anyone. She would naturally satisfy a lot of her comfort for others to rise because she sees the future in them.

d. **Lively and humorous**: Frederick, a famous psychologist who worked on Positive thinking explains that the greatest investment of positive thinkers is in their humor. They are not comedians, but they have drilled themselves so strongly that nothing sounds shocking to them. They don't believe anything is a big deal, and so, they can laugh it off. This ability to laugh it off gives them the vibe to handle any negative situation. Even in somber situations when everyone became quiet and full of worries, a positive thinking person would simply stand and declare 'come on, this isn't the end, toast to an undying struggle!" Soon enough, everyone joins in the party.

Ronald is a positive thinker who worked in California. He had a long list of friends to visit, people to meet every day and tasks to do before going to work. He often appears late to work due to these activities, and his boss soon got tired of it. She called him in and fired him one morning after she had issued series of warning. But the mesmerizing part was that everyone knew immediately, and they began to express their regret to see him go as he stepped out of her office. Many were already finding the right words to use with the always-happy guy who they would all have to see off now. 'I am so sorry about that' some were going to say, but he stunned them with his behavior. 'what is happening here, why is everyone getting so emotional? Is anyone going to buy me a drink at night or are you all going to sing me to bed?'. Everyone laughed. 'Sure, a drink at night'. They began to say till the whole room started to rebound with 'yeah, ah ah a drink at night!'. Ronald led them to party over what they would have chosen to be sad about.

e. **See the good sides of everything**: Besides their undying trust and hope in others, positive thinkers see the good side of everything only. Well, the engine room burnt and everyone began to think the company would be going in ruins soon. What does an optimistic manager do instead? Set up a meeting Engineering NGOs or similar corporations that may be willing to donate or loan the company enough funds to build back what they had lost. If not that, he could be planning big ideas to get funds from international investors that would never fail. So, he simply considers the inferno an opportunity and opportunity to build something bigger.

The same could be said about a student who got dismissed: it is just an opportunity to enroll elsewhere. A parent's death is for one to understand what life could seem without a parent and so on. When their world is beginning to look perfect and something crashes; they probably lost their spouse, job, car or kids, they do not despair about it for life. They simply remind themselves that losing some of these can help one to appreciate it better. They develop an automatic positive answer for everything. This is entirely different from the same way a pessimist would handle these case. And that is one value of positive thinking that cannot be overestimated.

f. **Can handle failure and rejection**: At least once in a lifetime, we all have to be rejected, insulted, hated and disrespected. It could be from those who loathe us, don't who care about us or those who are in a competition with us. Probably, we are bidding for the same job, same contract, or the same position as them. I wouldn't be surprised if any of them take to the press houses or social media to call me names, we all find a way to survive that. But the biggest rejection would call from our friends. If my best just took to social media to tell the world I have a devil that no one knew, I might find that hard to handle. You probably might too, because this is someone whom you have trusted completely. You have dined, danced, cried together and now they are letting you down in front of everyone. It may not even be a friend in your own case, it might be some significant like your son, spouse, mother or sister. It is as bad as placing you and your husband in a boxing ring, what do you do?

This is another position that being optimistic is the only thing that could keep you sane. You have certainly heard that people fail, shoot you in the dark and hurt you. but you can hardly be prepared for this. You must be full of hope and calm spirit. Laugh as much as you can, find other ways and forget everything someone is doing to bring you down. This is exactly what optimists do. It may be hard, but they recuperate, quickly. An experience like this can bring about depression, uncertainty, anger, and mental clutter. You may never progress in your career if you are trapped in the defeat that comes from a situation like this. You don't deserve that, and that is why you must try to think positively.

g. **Don't give up**: Even when everyone seems to hate a positively minded person, they do not give up on themselves. It is always nice to remember that if no one supports or understands you now, someone would come around to do it as long as you don't ever give up on yourself. Resilience is a skill that grows with your ability to maintain your ground. You must have seen how some of your friends maintained their ground when everyone thought they were saying thrash. Workers might dislike a director because she makes a thorough analysis of their action. Sometimes, they might be so bitter to the point that she could read it from their talks and reaction to it. A negatively minded person may become sad and downhearted. But as a director who understands her job, she must never give up. If everyone else hates you because they think you work too much, you must continue in spite of it.

If you live with your brother for instance, and he warned you not to mention a word of his rebellious life to his wife. You might do it when she asks, and at the end, he realizes and throws you out of the house. An optimist sees no reason to worry, they remain resilient and honest, and they go on finding solutions to the problems they see. This is not all.

h. **Appreciative**: how much do you appreciate other people? Even as the superior who cannot be messed with by anyone, do you spare time to tell your staff they did a good job? Sometimes, your staff are interested in their pay, but not as much as they want to hear 'good job boy, that's the spirit!'". It is a lubricant to the soul of anyone. It can drive them crazy enough to do double the job they are expected to do. It is okay to scream 'rubbish!' in their ears if you want them to understand that what they did was bad. But this also means you must learn to say 'that's awesome bud! Thumbs up Daniella!'

We all want to hear it but you may be unable to tell it if you are engrossed in your sadness and worry. In fact, you will find it hard to prove your satisfaction with a slight smile. Nobody wants you to be like that. You want them your friends, your family and your colleagues to tell you that you did a brilliant job too. So, you must learn to tell it to whoever earns it. Has your child done an awesome thing, tell him. Did he write his assignment well? Credit him. Did your staff handle the case well in your absence? Pat him. It can earn you a lot of respect and affection. It is also a sign of positivism. The people around you understand that you are positive and you always have some good words for them at the end of the day, that is if they did the job well. If you were in their shoes, how would you handle jobs like that?

i. Truth: Why should I lie about this? Positive minds never really understand the reason they should lie about anything. In most cases, they had good minds and good thoughts about others, so, when anything goes wrong, they see only reasons they should tell it as it is. They might find some euphemistic method of presenting the story, but certainly, the truth is the truth to them. This is the exact reason your kid will return from school and tell you he was mocked by his friends. Why? he refused to cheat in the test they had and he had the lowest grade. He didn't feel bad of course, and he would love to be upright again. You can tell that your child is growing with a positive mind and it becomes your job to encourage him to improve that mindset.

Telling the truth isn't always simple. Sometimes, the upshot of telling the truth might be disastrous. You smuggled the company's machine home and it got spoilt before you could return it. You caught some key officers planning how to pull the wool over the company's executives. You realize the danger in saying all of these things, and if you were a pessimist, your brain would immediately remind you the danger of leaking out what you know. As an optimist however, your brain would stay glued to the positive aspects. Wouldn't it be great if they stopped searching for the machine because they knew I had it already? Isn't it safer for the company if they knew some of their team were have things up their

82

sleeve? Thoughts like these can make you fearless, and a life like this is what positive thinking brings to being.

Advantages of Positive thinking

Now that you know the key features of positive thinking. The most important thing is to find out why you should start thinking positively too. What do you stand to gain by thinking positively? I am sure you would have realized some from the discussion we were having up there. But in details, here are the advantages of thinking positively.

a.   **Life span increase**: Positive thinking has almost all the features that can help a person live longer. Starting with a clear mind. You don't have to hide things in your head, you don't have to hold grudges too. There is happiness and rest of mind. I remember telling you that anyone who has a positive mindset would likely laugh more, joke about everything and feel no reason to hold rejection or failure to their heart. Another interesting fact is that you will pay more attention to your health, drugs and food since your mind is not overly preoccupied by your problems. You spend some time out with friends, there is no reason you shouldn't have fun and live longer.

b.   **Absence of Mental Clutters**: Struggling to capture many things in your head at once is what causes mental clutter. As a lively person, an optimist has a happy-go-lucky style of handling crisis that makes it seem like nothing was ever a problem actually. A positively minded person may not even have to use the journal technique (remember what that is?) when they have pressing troubles, rather, their friends are always willing to suggest solutions to their problems. Since most problems are shared, it doesn't clutter in their head. Given that you can handle rejection or failure without making a fuss too, you will not feel the urge to jump into a terrible decision or fear failure. Your pasts, your presents, everything that you used to worry about becomes your source of courage and fun.

c.   **Lower levels of distress**: If you have a positive mindset, distress is hardly one of the problems you would face. You could still have a lot of problems to attend to. The files at work, the tales from your wayward brother. The old granny and her request and then, there are the kids. But no matter the height of all of these troubles, you can't ever be distressed by them. why? because you are always handling everything with fun. Let me show how it works:

Mom: (Calls cellphone) hi sonny, I need you to come over and supervise the telephone company here.
Me: Oh that, I will send my cat.
Mom: (laughs) did you hear me, you brute. Does a cat supervise you at work?
Me: (muse) Yeah mama, my kid boss is pretty like a pussy cat.
Mom: (sighs in amusement) That's your problem, not mine. Who oversees the phone firm?
Me: (curious) You really don't want the cat?
Mom: (makes a face) A lion will do.
Me: Done. (smiles into the face)
Mom: What? (pleasant surprise)
Me: My wife is a lioness, she'll be there.

Mom: I'll eat you up if I smell you in my area
Me: I'm a ripe apple. I'll be there next week, but she will see about the supervision.
Mom: Ok then, bye darling! (laughs again)

Just look at that? how'd you find the conversation? Even though I may not be at her home at the promised period, I may find some other excuse to keep her excited yet. If you handle all of your daily problems that way, can you ever be distressed?

d. **Better work results**: Since you began handling issues with a laissez faire lifestyle, you can't ever run into problems. Everything seems so simple that you have no trouble moving your job further. With a positive mindset, you feel the vibe to do more, you also have enough jokes going around the staff members such that they keep working without getting tired. You are much more relaxed and comfortable, so you can easily focus on the job at hand. I have already proven to you that mistakes are avoided and the job is faster when there is much more concentration.

e. **Mind freedom**: The major reason you are a cause of headache to yourself is probably the secrets that lurk in your heart but you cannot share with anyone. You are usually quiet and you feel uncomfortable with everyone too. Such a life won't be yours if you have think positively. You would find it easy to share everything that bothers you with friends without making a fuss or making sound very huge. You would not leave people with mysteries, they won't keep wondering why you live an awkward life around them. Rather, you would leave them with love and sweet memories each time you walk away.

f.   **Ability to handle problems better**: A huge advantage of being a positive thinker is that you can handle problems a lot better than you would as a neutral or negative thinker. Your problems would not appear like problems to you, they would seem a series of tasks that you only need to get out of your way. That is not all, you would mix problems with a normal life in a way that you would not be able to discern them as problems or even brood over them. when you eventually have problems in your hand, you are often clear-headed enough to think properly and patiently produce the solution.

the pasts can't hurt you.

g.   **Psychological and physical healthiness**: As a whole, positively minded people can be proud of a healthy life. Psychologically, their thoughts are always clear, straightforward and not cluttered. They also ensure they are not depressed about anything. They have reasons to worry once in a while, but before long, they lose the effects of worrying in an outburst about other issues. They also pay enough attention to their food. Hardly would they their skip meals or take ill-nourished foods. Therefore, there is a low chance of diabetes, ulcer, nutrient shortage, among other diet complications. They don't lose their sleep over anything either, so insomnia is out of the options. Also, despite their age, they would always pick interest in simple workouts. Here is exactly what I told you about grandma and grandpa. Imagine waking and sleeping in happiness. You don't even have anything to worry about because nothing gets to you.

h. **Reduced risk of Cardiovascular problems**: If just for this, you should consider it necessary to think positively. Thinking positively connotes that you don't worry about things to the point of heaving a sigh unconsciously and experiencing various cardiovascular diseases. It would be easy for you to relate with others and your health remains in a top condition. Usually, diseases that can be generated from depressions, sighing or overthinking have a low chance of affecting you. Hypertensions inclusive.

i. **Respect and love of others**: Do you know you deserve to be loved and respected by others? Right, you do. But have you imagined that the easiest way to earn the love and respect of others is by giving it to them? Well, don't be surprised. According to Frederick (2004), a fact that most people do not understand about love is that they need to give it out in order to be given. You have to pay attention to others around you, listen to them, show them that you care and they would be more than willing to die for you. You might want to say that you have given love and respect to a lot of people who didn't you it to you in turn. Well, that is absolutely possible. You must remember that your care would be unrequited in some instances. Rather, some other people would show you love and then you decide whether you want to reciprocate their care. The most important point is that you remain in the circle.

Have you got the balls to think positively for the rest of your life? Come on, it is a great habit, and you don't want to be anything else!

Chapter 7: The Importance of Meditation.

We have talked about thinking all day, but we cannot stop talking about 'thinking' without making references to Medication. What is that? According to Madhav Goyal, Meditation is about training the mind actively to understand itself and its environment. In essence, it is a deliberate attempt by a person to direct his mind towards revealing everything that goes on in it, and its immediate environment. You can picture yourself trying to control your mind to do it.

Similarly, Herbert Benson is a famous psychologist who believes that meditation is a solitary practice in which you quietly stay by yourself for a calculated period of time, you focus on your breath, and pay attention to your thoughts. Basically, it is one of the psychotherapeutic methods you use to connect yourself, your mind and your environment, and it has advantages much more than you can imagine. Till date, research is still ongoing on its effectiveness and achievement, although meditation was never meant to achieve benefits, it is a simple mind cleansing exercises. To Buddhists, the primary value of meditation is to liberate the mind of the practitioner from thoughts that it has no control over.

From David Lynch Foundation records, we observe that meditation is a habit that has been in existence for ages.

It's been known across old cultures and people like the Indian, Chinese, Egyptians and so on. At that time, it always had something to do with religion unlike today when it has little regard with religion. Today, it is still common among some communities America, India and a few other places. Basically, it is an appealing attempt to clear your mind, alter consciousness of the body and relax your soul. There are various types of meditation, but they usually involve the same method. So how is it done?

Steps to Meditation:

a. **Sit**: From everyone you might ask, sitting is the first step to proper meditation. You cannot meditate excellently while standing, bending or using some other position. Although, some types of meditation would require you to move. (don't be in a rush, I will tell you all about them). you could use a meditation chair, cushion or as most people do, the floor. The direct alternative to sitting is to lie on the floor.

b. **Shut your eyes**: The next thing to do after sitting or lying on the floor is to slam your eyes shut. Not just your eyes, but most parts of your body. Allow them all to rest and make no attempt to use them or channel your energy into any of them. Use masks that can prevent you from opening your eyelids if you have to. There are specialized masks for this activity.

c. **Read your body**: Pay thorough attention to your body. Without raising any part of your body, feel each of them. You need not channel any energy into them, just try to feel them. Is every part of your body comfortable? Your back, your arms, your ankles, leg and neck. You can feel the comfort of them all without adjusting your position at all. If anyone seems inconvenient, adjust that part to increase its convenience.

d. **Breathe**: Now pay attention to your breath. You do not even have to help yourself breathe. Don't increase or decrease the pace of your regular breath, just pay attention to the rhythm, the sound and the pace of your breath as if all you can do for yourself at the moment. Maybe it really is though. If you notice that your mind drifts to some other topics, problems or some other thoughts you had earlier, call it to order. Force it to return to your present situation and focus on breathing.

That is all you have to do. Simple! Isn't it? Trust me, it isn't simple for anyone, especially a beginner. You may begin with about 3 to 5 minutes on a daily basis. You would have to maintain your position, your mood, and the state of your mind throughout the period. After that, you would have to lose yourself in semi-consciousness, and then you could think about specific things. You will understand better when we discuss the types of meditation. Now, let's see, what are the different types of Meditation that we can have?

The Types of Meditation

1. **Mindfulness Meditation**: In the words of Alice Milton (2019), 'mindfulness meditation is the most common type of meditation in the West'. It is coined from Indian Sayagyi U Ba Khin tradition where its

model has been in practice for over 2500 years. In order to practice this, you must be relaxed enough to reflect on anything. You can actually practice this anywhere; at school, home, kitchen, et cetera. As long as you are calm and relaxed enough to maintain silence and stability for a while. It is also necessary to be at a spot that no one could break into your thoughts all through.

After you must have settled to begin, the next basic step is to shut your eyes. Thereafter, pay attention to your nearest environment. You do not have to channel your energy to anything, just lay relaxed and begin to feel your skin. Feel your hands, legs, neck and head. Feel the silent wind blow through them, and ensure they are all comfortable. Prominently, you shouldn't forget to check how you are breathing. Every one of these without flickering a finger or blinking an eyelid.

After you have done all of these, begin to see into your own heart. Remember not to input any energy or try to control it at all. You should also remember that you may see nothing if you do not allow your body to completely relax and focus on your breathing only. Allow your mind to do its wandering. Then remain still as it brings scenes and images into your heart. Watch it all and make no contribution, just the way you would see scenes at a cinema and make no effort to influence it. Your mind would probably reflect on the past events in your life, the present and those that made you restless before you started. For example, your mind could give you clues on the interaction you have had with a former staff of your company. How you insulted him and fired him for

91

breaking one of your hallowed regulations. Your mind might begin to suggest that you shouldn't have punished to a stage of dismissal. He could still be instrumental to your company's development, et cetera. Take mental note of all of these, it is your mind proffering suggestions to you.

You will make a great mistake by forcing this scene off your mind immediately. It would mean that you would appreciate and understand little of how much your own mind could offer in your life choices. You would also end up being troubled as earlier rather than have a cleansed heart. You may however set a timer for the period you intend to use. The instant the wail of the alarm breaks into your thoughts, you should return to full consciousness. One unique advantage of this system is that you need no teacher to practice it, and it can be used to solve a specific problem. For example; depression, indecision, and so forth.

Basically, two types of mindfulness meditation are known:

i. Mindfulness based stress reduction (MBSR)
ii. Mindfulness based cognitive therapy (MBCT)

2. **Movement meditation**: Movement Meditation is the direct opposite of Mindfulness meditation in a single regard. It involves movement while mindfulness meditation requires complete stillness. You might wonder, how can one meditate on the move? Well, it is possible, and you can do it too. It is only that you cannot do it if you do not have a natural flair for stillness. You

should be someone who finds pleasure in moving about, taking leisure strolls, and hanging around a garden.

Then, you feel the idea of sitting while to meditate really sucks. This would be your thing if you fancy the Chinese Qigong too. Sometimes, you remain on a sport and move parts of your body, but in most cases, you move from one spot to another. Your meditation is entirely guided by your movements in this case. This means that the goal is not to travel far, it is a simple walk in which your mind pays prompt attention to the feelings in your feet. Your heart beats with each movement and so does your thoughts. The interesting thing about this type of meditation is that it requires no special instrument for practice (no mask, no couch), instead it can help you positively contribute to your environment.

There are numerous types of movement meditation. It's about how you choose to view it. The basic ones are:

a. Walking or Running: This happens when you take a leisure walk in the garden, silent street or your favorite touring spot. You take measured steps that rhymes with your heartbeat as you walk. How do you know when it rhymes? Study, pay attention. As you repeat this exercise and pay little attention to other things in your environment, you would soon find yourself lost in the subconscious meditation realm. Remember not to interrupt it unless the alarm does.

b. Dancing: It is interesting to learn that one can meditate while dancing. You can do it if you are the type who listens to a favorite song for a long period. Elysha Lekin reports that in most cases, people who listen to a favorite song, especially if it is a slow beat music, are often lost in meditation while listening to the music. For example, you might begin to dance to your slow beat music in steps. Slowly moving your body to the rhythm of the song in calculated steps. Unconsciously, you would hear the beats and you would soon be lost in its rhythm. You would focus on your feet movement and gradually drift into thinking. It is always advised to gather a playlist of favorite songs when you desire to use this method. This is to ensure that the song doesn't stop while you are halfway in your meditation.

c. <u>Yoga</u>: Yoga is a pack of activities that can bolster your personality. At the end of your daily yoga practice, one of the activities you could try out is meditation.

d. <u>Cleaning</u>: since cleaning often require you to repeat a movement, it could lead to meditation. You can easily begin to meditate as you stretch your hands or legs forward and backward.

3. **Spiritual Meditation**: A spiritual meditation is any meditation that holds spiritual significance to the participant. You are doing it because it is the customary method of meditating in your religion. As I have mentioned earlier, most religions Chakra, Hinduism, Christianity, Daoism) have a method of meditation they each adopted. This method may be practiced in the religious home or at home. A peculiar feature of the spiritual meditation is that each of these methods often require another ingredient. This may include Frankincense, sage, cedar, palo santo, incense and so on.

In particular, chakra meditation is practiced in India. A method that also focuses on bringing balance and relaxation to all of the chakras. What are the chakras? They are the seven parts of the human body believed to be the specific parts that are sources of spiritual power and energy in the body.

4. **Focused Meditation**: Focused meditation is another famous type of meditation. You engage in this when you have a specific target to meditate upon. It can also help you to develop the ability to focus on a problem at a time. Usually, you could use all your sense organs when practicing this type of meditation. It requires a lot of silence and attention, and it can be triggered by anything you do not expect. For instance, the gentle breeze blowing on your bare foot, the candle you watch flicker, the breeze blowing through your face, et cetera. The major difficulty with this method is that it is always hard to maintain your focus. You'd be tempted to steal a look at your right or your left.

5. **Mantra Meditation**: Mantra Meditation is common among religious communities, though it is not necessarily constricted to them. It is the habit of meditating by repeating certain words or mantra. These words are often for assurance, and they are accompanied by another type of meditation, usually action. It is often geared towards a particular motive. For instance, if I shut my eyes and rest my spirit in a mindfulness motivation, I may begin to repeat some Mantra such as "rest my soul, rest..." repeating such mantra often bear no magical influence on the

meditation, however, repeating it can instill it into the mind and spirit of the person who practices it.

6. **Guided Meditation**: If you are not sure about practicing any of this meditation yourself, you might decide to hire a teacher or guide. Hiring a teacher increases the chances of learning faster and learning in a well-planned/controlled environment. So, you might want to give that a trial. It doesn't matter the medication type you have hired a guide for, it will be regarded as 'guided meditation' as long as you have hired a guide.

Having considered the unalike kinds of Meditation, we should begin to ask ourselves now: why is meditation even important?

Benefits of meditation

Meditation is ideal for the following reasons:

a. **Lower Blood pressure**: The major cause of blood pressure is the restlessness and troubles a person goes through on a daily basis. If you are the type who leaves home before your kids wake and you are not coming till everyone on the street is asleep, you are prone to this. In particular, if you go through so much stress and series of disturbing activities that lead to tension, you are highly likely to suffer blood pressure. Sparing some time to meditate can however help you to avoid such situations. Regular meditation leads to regular relaxation, and relaxation is a certain way to clear off your worries.

b. **Relaxation**: If you have been working hard in recent times and you can't afford to take a proper vacation just yet, meditation is definitely the solution. Your average meditation takes between 10 to 30 minutes a day. That is a period you could spend in your bed. You are spending this on a rest too, the only difference is that you are deliberately reflecting in your rest this time.

c. **Lower Cortisol levels**: Do you remember what you learnt about Cortisol? It is easily triggered by anything and it causes sadness. As much as you allow it. You can avoid cortisol release or trim it to a relatively low level by meditating. In the first place, you are relaxed, not worried. So, nothing would naturally trigger cortisol. Along these lines, your cortisol level will not rise during your meditation period because your mind and brain are actively engaged in an activity that contradicts depression; reflection. So, your cortisol level would be stemmed if you regularly meditate.

d. **Feelings of Well-being**: Happiness, confidence and rest of mind would naturally overwhelm your spirit if you spend enough time meditating. The feelings of well-being that you take on from your morning meditation can lift your spirit as you step in the day's works. If you started meditation after running all of the day's shows and struggles, you can expect impacts too. All of the day's problems that linger in your mind would gradually wipe off, replaced with an ecstatic feeling of peace and purity. Picking up a feeling of well-being can help you handle all of your leadership tasks, your relationship with everyone at home and work, and each problem as it surfaces.

e. **Problem Solving**: Talking about problems, the need to solve them is sometimes the reason we try meditation. You would remember it doesn't mean so much to the Buddhists, but to average men who may not practice it for religious purpose, this may be a problem solving avenue. How? Your mind might pick on the problem that bothers you and meditate on it at length. From the meditation, you could find the solution to the riddle that surround the problem. Remember that you must make mental note of each statement in the discourse. Also, you would be able to think better about the problem the instant your mind is decluttered and free by the meditation.

f. **Mental clutter**: Just as you might guess, meditation is a fierce method of method of battling mental clutters. Your brain and mind becomes clear, relaxed and open enough to face a new set of problems. In fact, your brain seems so refreshed that it doesn't seem to have handled problems earlier. This is one of the numerous benefits of meditation.

g. **Preserves aging brain**: meditation does a world of benefits to the human brain. It helps to the human brain busy, thereby preventing it from default mode network, it could result in changes in the volume of the brain and among other benefits, it could help you cure addiction. Preservation of an aging brain is one other benefit that cannot be overestimated. From various records, it has been proven that meditation helps you remember scenes in your mind's eyes. So, proper medication could help you recollect most of the talks you had with others, most of the words you used and unlike others, what each conversation was about. This skill can make you everyone's favorite at old age, as they understand that they won't have to repeat the same conversation again.

h. **Anti-depressant**: Among other benefits, meditation has also proven to be a cure for depression. It is a kind of reflection that stops depression. When you allow your mind to express all that it has thought through, you would realize that you need not be depressed about some certain things, and you would simply work on getting better with them. On a similar note, the thoughts of the job you lost, the death of a loved one the efforts of your life would definitely stem up in your meditation process. Therefore, you are more likely to have poured out your what is in your earth in your depression. There is no fear of depression again.

i. **It can improve your concentration and attention**: as you would expect, your ability to focus on whatever you are doing would be improved. If you are the type who would certainly keep your wandering around other issues when you should concentrate and proffer solutions to one, this might just be your perfect avenue to learn how to focus on one problem at a time.

Gee! I have empowered you with so many details about medication that the only thing I expect is that you would pick it up soonest. Is that a 'yeah' I hear?

Chapter 8: Practicing Positive Mindfulness

Mindfulness is the habit of focusing on the present and making no attempt to judge it. It basically refers to your recognition of where you are, what you are doing as well as your condition without making attempts to judge or become overwhelmed by it. For example, you are mindful of the fact that you are in your office and you have some urgent problems you must attend to. You are at home with an eye on the kid, the other in the kitchen and your mind in the drawing room. You are mindful of the need to be in all of these places at almost the same time. You are aware of the recent disaster you suffered at work and you made no attempt to judge your effort as either excellent or terrible.

It started in spiritual and religious communities across the eastern world and thanks to Jon Kabat-Zin of the University of Massachusetts Medical School, it is becoming relatively popular in the US, and of course, the West today. He has initiated various programs and written books to that end.

Positive Mindfulness is a broader term however. It describes your realization about yourself and how you make exigent efforts to improve your presence in the community. You realize where you are and you see the need to get better. You bear a positive picture of yourself and your impacts in the community. In essence, this is about moving from a neutral position of existence to a positive position of impact, influence and dominance. From the position of a person struggling to become aware and hang on to a community, to someone who's aware of his community and would continue to make active efforts in developing his community. Though, you need to begin with mindfulness.

Positive mindfulness can be applied in many areas of the human life. Your children need a lot of it in the classroom. You need to exhibit it as parents, you need to learn how to build positive mindfulness in the face of anxiety as well as depression. Importantly, you should understand how you can apply this at work too. You will find the technique to do all of these in the coming line, but just before that, I would want you to see some of the benefits, or reasons you really should commit yourself to positive mindfulness.

Benefits of Positive Mindfulness

a. **It helps you out of overthinking**: Rather than stare into space every time, lost in thoughts and unsure about where you are or what you are doing, you would be more stable. You would find it a lot more comfortable to focus on reality and give your current situation your best shot.
b. **Mindfulness helps you maintain concentration**: I cannot overemphasize the value of concentration to you. Your concentration rate can, to a large extent determine how good or bad the jobs you did were. How well you took care of your kids and how well you are compelling yourself to provide solutions to the problems at hand.

c. **Mindfulness relives stress and anxiety**: The exact reason you were worried and stress was that you had too much in your plate. Your attention was drifting from a near problem to the next and then its distant nephew. You are worried about the hook, the boat and then the sea. One certain way out of this emotional chaos is to engage in positive mindfulness.

d. **Mindfulness improves improve rest**: with the awareness that you cannot change your present and you cannot control what happens in the imaginary realm, mindfulness is your best bet. It grounds you in the present and assist you to realize your powers which you may afterwards, apply to your multifaceted life.

e. **Mindfulness increases your sexual and marital life**: If you are the emotional type who connects your sexual encounters with your emotion, it is important for you to mindful than not to be. Being mindful means you are focused on nothing but the present as you enjoy your sexual experience. It also means you would enjoy an amorous relationship with your lover since you do not focus on other experiences, especially those in the pasts and those that linger in your thoughts, causing fear and unrest.

f. **It helps you do better at work**: The last on the list, mindfulness aids you to become an inexhaustible worker. You become prolific, comfortable and focused on the future. You are also concerned about the present, the reality than fantastic imaginations. This enables you to focus more on the job at hand and give it your best shot.

Practicing positive mindfulness is not trouble-free however. It has a lot of advantages with a few demerits.

But the real problem is that it could be hard to start. It could be hard to realize the areas that need to be boosted with positive mindfulness. It could be challenging to start and worst of all, to keep the practice going. This is why I will expansively discuss the different techniques to achieve this in the next few pages. Ready? Awesome!

Techniques to practice positive mindfulness

a. **Sacrifice** some space and time: Imagine having a silent place in your house where you walk into every morning. Once you get in there, everyone realizes they should neither call your name disturb you in anyway till you get yourself out. Can you sacrifice a space like? It is the perfect community for anyone to start. You will have to make out time out. The least you would need is 10 minutes daily. Why? To guarantee effectiveness of the mindfulness. You can go on to spend 30 minutes though. As long as you are sure you could be consistent with that time frame.

b. **Invite yourself to the party**: the instant you have set your quiet place and you are set to start, your first task is to commit yourself. You need to bring your mind and memory to what you do. This is not because you need to remember whatever you do here; actually, you don't. Rather, it is to guarantee your full concentration. You want to make sure that your body and soul are with you, one is not yearning to listen to the news on TV or wondering if the scotch is burning off already. Summarily, see to it that you are completely here.

c. **Listen, don't comment**: The next most important instruction is to listen. The moment you were walking into your positive mindfulness practice room is your past. The moment you woke is in the past, as well as every second that went before now. You need to take your mind off every period that's in the past already. Be concerned about one period, now. Let your thoughts choose what flows in and out of them, and focus on your breath. You will have to focus on all of your sense organs too. which of them is reporting to you, and what is it saying?

d. **Be**: Even when you can hear the low sound in the atmosphere, the tiny prickle somewhere in your skin, the tiny droplet of water navigating your spine downwards, you must do nothing. You should remain as calm and still as possible. Try not to even turn your head or raise it.

e. **Don't jump into the future**: In all frankness, there is no reason to rush into the future. Whether you desire to be there or not, you'd have to be there sometime. Why should you rush it then? Relax. It's a good thing that you have stopped thinking about the past. But now, you must take your mind off the future too. In case you are wondering, 'what then will I think about?' I am glad to tell you that your answer is the objective of this exercise; spend some time to think about nothing. I understand you want to be worried about the future but you must take your eyes off the timer, the alarm would sound anyway.

f. **Let your mind wander**: Now listen to your wandering heart. It will naturally express your thoughts, talks, actions and the intrinsic motivation you have given yourself. There may be voices shouting 'this is really bad; I shouldn't have done it!'. You might hear some telling you that you did a great job. You should take a mental note of all of these experiences. But ensure that you do not pass your own judgment, include your own comments or wipe the thoughts off in impatience.

g. **Don't be hard on yourself**: I must inform you that our mind is tricky and unreasonably unpredictable. It may choose to evaluate actions you have performed long before now. It may choose to open your recent decisions and rather than laud you for the positive entries, it slams you the errors you made in that decision. You need to understand that this is all part of the process, and as such, you should not react to it. don't get yourself worked up over this.

h. **Return to reality**: the thinking phase is the longest of all phases. It requires you to travel the world in your head. You would likely feel like you have just met a doctor, a counsellor, a mother or a brother too. Then again, it would all end the instant your body feels saturated. You feel enough tranquility or the alarm is sounding. Feel at ease to return to reality and remember that blaming yourself over any of those thoughts does not change anything. Pick the points you can from the lessons you have just learnt, and start off to a beautiful morning!

<u>Tips to enjoy your positive mindfulness</u>

1. **Identify areas to change**: You could have a speedy, and much more positive mindfulness if you identify the areas you'd like to change. For instance, everyone thinks you are too slow at your job and you desire to change that part, you have identified an area already. By the period you enter into your meditation room, there are

high chances that your mind will pick on this area and discuss it extensively. It will share you contrasting ideas on the problem and at the end, you will certainly have stronger insights on how you can help yourself better.

2. **Practice your daily pronouncements**: you may consider using a mantra to boost your meditation. This is done by repeating certain affirmations. Mostly, to improve your overall confidence, patience and ability to handle multitasks. Some religious and spiritual communities recommend certain mantras, but as an individual, it is ideal to make up your own mantra yourself. You could try words such as 'I am going to win today', 'success must come'. 'I will make this happen', et cetera.

Be open to humor: Due to your positivism, you must learn to be open to humor wherever you find yourself. Laughing when you can and putting smile on people's faces can be the ideal boost you need to handle your own problems. In fact, I'd tell you to implant a permanent smile on your face. and ensure you attempt to practice positive self-talk. What is that? Positive Self talk describes the habit of saying good or positive things about yourself. You may tell yourself you believe in yourself. Remind yourself that you will get on to work and you are going to make the rest of your life, the best of your life.

Conclusion

In this book, I have paid a thorough attention to one of the biggest problems on planet earth; overthinking. I quoted instances of overthinking and I attached the major causes of this problem. In fact, you will find all the tell-tale signs of overthinking and the reasons why a person who overthinks may not get help early enough.

Then, we looked into mental clutter, its causes and the feasible effects. If you read on, you will find out how to declutter your thoughts in this book, as well as how to create good habits. That is not all, I took a meticulous period to provide information on two other phenomenal issues: positive and negative thinking. You must have been amazed to read some thoroughly detailed facts about those two concepts. I'm really eager to know, are you going to be trying out any type of meditation sometime? Would you still need some help?

What else did you come across? You definitely wouldn't miss the concept of meditation and its effects, as well as the how to start positive mindfulness. We are going to be discussing something different in my next book. Kindly leave a great comment if you enjoyed this, till I write you again; stay positive!

CPSIA information can be obtained
at www.ICGtesting.com
Printed in the USA
BVHW092149220221
600778BV00008B/934

9 781914 104909